THE LAST OF
THE THREE MUSKETEERS

Borgo Press Drama Translations by FRANK J. MORLOCK

Plays by ALEXANDRE DUMAS

Anthony
The Count of Monte Cristo, Part One
The Count of Monte Cristo, Part Two
The Count of Monte Cristo, Part Three
The Count of Monte Cristo, Part Four
The Last of the Three Musketeers; or, The Prisoner of the Bastille
Napoléon Bonaparte
Richard Darlington
The San Felice
The Three Musketeers
Urbain Grandier and the Devils of Loudon
The Whites and the Blues

THE LAST OF THE THREE MUSKETEERS

OR,
THE PRISONER
OF THE BASTILLE:
A PLAY IN FIVE ACTS

ALEXANDRE DUMAS

Translated and Adapted by Frank J. Morlock

THE BORGO PRESS
MMXI

THE LAST OF THE THREE MUSKETEERS

Copyright © 2011 by Frank J. Morlock

FIRST EDITION

Published by Wildside Press LLC

www.wildsidebooks.com

DEDICATION

For My Friends,

Ron Sanders and Jane Eaton

CONTENTS

CHARACTERS 9
ACT I, Scene 1 11
ACT I, Scene 2 53
ACT II, Scene 3. 67
ACT II, Scene 4. 111
ACT III, Scene 5 149
ACT IV, Scene 6 185
ACT IV, Scene 7 215
ACT V, Scene 8. 217
ACT V, Scene 9. 251
ABOUT THE AUTHOR 261

CHARACTERS

King Louis XIV
Marchiali
D'Artagnan
Aramis
Athos
Porthos
Fouquet
Basiemaux de Montlezun
De Vardes
Saint-Aignan
François
An Usher
A Courtier
Louise de la Vallière
Anne of Austria
Madame Henriette
Madame de Chevreuse
Aure de Montalais
Athénaïs de Tonnay-Charente
A Female Servant

ACT I
SCENE 1

The Louvre.

COURTIERS

(waiting for the King to rise)

A PAGE

The King, gentlemen.

ALL

The King! The King!

KING

(entering)

Good morning, gentlemen—the night was good—I wish I could say as much for the Cardinal—any news of him?

COURTIER

I left his Eminence's, Sire—I spent part of the night—

KING

Well, sir?

COURTIER

There were two crises during which the doctor thought His Eminence was going to pass—

KING

Gentlemen, you won't be astonished that I am going to abridge this morning's reception—I would never forgive myself if Cardinal Mazarin were to die without, one last time exposing my gratitude for the services he rendered me. Goodbye, gentlemen.

(The Courtiers bow and leave.)

USHER

Your Majesty's carriage is ready.

KING

Go to Her Majesty, the Queen Mother and ask her if she will accompany me to His Eminence!

QUEEN

(entering)

Useless, my son—the Cardinal can no longer receive anyone.

KING

Not even me?

QUEEN

For this last ten minutes is seems he has completely lost consciousness.

KING

Who told you that, Madame?

QUEEN

A certain Mr. Colbert, who is from his house and says he has an important paper to deliver to you on the Cardinal's behalf.

KING

Where is he?

QUEEN

In the Diana Salon.

KING

Show in Mr. Colbert who comes in behalf of His Eminence.

USHER

Sire, while Mr. Colbert was waiting, a courier from His Eminence came to tell him that the Cardinal had regained consciousness and was asking for him.

KING

And he left?

USHER

Saying "Deliver this paper to the King—but only to the King himself, I won't be slow to return."

KING

That paper?

USHER

Here it is.

KING

Give it here.

(hearing noise in the gallery)

Oh-oh! Who's coming to us in such a great uproar?

QUEEN

Either I'm mistaken or it must be your Finance Minister.

KING

Oh! Mr. Fouquet.

FOUQUET

(entering)

Himself, sire! And you see a desperate man—not having arrived in time for Your Majesty's Rising—Madame.

(bowing to the Queen)

KING

You know, Mr. Fouquet, that His Eminence is badly ill?

FOUQUET

Yes, Sire, I know that—the news reached me this morning at Vaux—and it was so pressing that I left the very instant I learned of it.

KING

You were at Vaux this morning, sir?

FOUQUET

(pulling a magnificent watch form his pocket)

I left there an hour and a half ago, Sire.

KING

An hour and a half? You came from Vaux to here in an hour and a half, sir?

FOUQUET

I understand, Sire, Your Majesty doubts my word; but if I came this way, it's truly by miracle: They sent me four pairs of very fast horses from England. They were harnessed four abreast and I tried them this morning. We got from Vaux to the Louvre in an hour and a half.

QUEEN

Those are some marvelous horses, sir!

FOUQUET

They were made for Kings and not for subjects, Madame.

QUEEN

Yet you are not King, so far as I know, Mr. Fouquet?

FOUQUET

No, Madame! But the horses are only waiting for a sign from His Majesty to enter the stables of the Louvre, and if I permitted myself to try them, it was only for fear of offering to the King something that was not marvelous.

QUEEN

You know, Mr. Fouquet, it's not the custom in the court of France for a subject to offer something to his King—

FOUQUET

I was hoping, Madame, that my love for His Majesty, my incessant desire to please him, would serve as a counterweight to reasons of etiquette, besides, it was not a present I was offering, it was a tribute I was paying—

KING

Mr. Fouquet, I thank your intention for indeed, I love fine horses; but you know quite well, I am not rich—you know it better than anyone. My Minister of Finance. Even if I wished it, I couldn't purchase such an expensive team of horses.

FOUQUET

Luxury is the virtue of Kings—it's through luxury they are more than other men—it's by luxury they resemble God. With luxury a King nourishes his subjects and honors them—under the sweet warmth of luxury. Kings give rise to the luxury of individuals a source of riches to the people. The King, by accepting these incomparable horses would have stung the various of horse breeders in our country:—this emulation would have been profitable to all. But the King is silent and consequently I am condemned.

KING

(who to give himself proper demeanor has unfolded the paper and glanced at it)

Ah, my God!

QUEEN

What's wrong, my son?

KING

From the Cardinal—it was really from the Cardinal this paper came?

QUEEN MOTHER

You heard the usher affirm it.

KING

Read, Madame.

QUEEN

(reading)

A donation—

FOUQUET

A donation?

KING

Yes—on the point of death, the Cardinal makes a donation to me of all his wealth.

QUEEN

Forty millions! Ah, my son—this is a beautiful deed on the part of the Cardinal and it is really going to contradict all those evil rumors—forty millions amassed slowly and which will return at a single stroke to the treasury—he's a faithful subject and a true Christian.

KING

(To Fouquet)

Why look, sir—it's not to be believed.

FOUQUET

Yes, Sire—I see perfectly—a donation and in order—

QUEEN

You must reply, Sire—you must reply at once.

KING

And say what, Madame?

QUEEN

Why that you are grateful to the Cardinal and that you accept. Isn't that your opinion, sir?

FOUQUET

I ask your pardon, Madame, but my opinion is that His Majesty express thanks; but—

KING

But what?

FOUQUET

But that he not accept….

QUEEN

Why's that?

FOUQUET

You yourself said it, Madame—because Kings ought not to accept presents from their subjects.

QUEEN

Hey, sir—instead of dissuading the King from receiving this present—observe to His Majesty, you whose duty it is—that these forty millions are a fortune.

FOUQUET

It's precisely because forty millions are a fortune, Madame, that I will say to the King—Sire, if it's not decent for Your Majesty to accept horses worth 20,000 pounds from a subject, it is dishonorable for him to owe his fortune to a subject rumored to be less scrupulous in the choice of means which contributed to the edifice of this fortune.

QUEEN

It doesn't behoove you, sir, to give a lesson to the King—instead procure him forty millions to replace those you are making him lose.

FOUQUET

(bowing)

The King shall have them when he wishes, Madame—

QUEEN

Yes, by pressuring the people.

FOUQUET

Eh! Weren't they pressured, Madame, when they were made to sweat out the forty millions given by this act—? Moreover, the King asked me my opinion—that's it. Let His Majesty demand my assistance, it would be the same—

QUEEN

Come, come, accept, my son. You are above rumors and interpretations.

FOUQUET

Refuse, Sire—so long as a King lives, he has no other than his conscience—no other judge than his will—but once dead, it will be posterity that applauds or accuses.

KING

Thanks, Mother! Thanks, Mr. Fouquet!

QUEEN

Well—what have you decided, my son?

FOUQUET

Mr. Fouquet, take this donation and return it to the family of Cardinal Mazarin, who must be in great anxiety. I thank His Eminence from the depth of my heart, but—

FOUQUET and the QUEEN

But?

KING

But I refuse.

FOUQUET

(rushing up and kissing the King's hand)

Sire, I don't know what your reign will be like, but the omens are good.

(he leaves)

QUEEN

My son, you just let slip an opportunity that you'll never have again.

KING

Madame, no one will accuse me of partiality to Mr. Fouquet, whom I detest instinctively and without knowing why—but this time, I am compelled to say he gave me truly royal counsel.

QUEEN

If that's the way it is, my son, I have only to withdraw and leave you to your good conscience—but I doubt that it will sustain you in place of forty millions it just cost you.

(she leaves)

USHER

(entering)

Sire, Mr. Colbert that Your Majesty was just asking for has returned to the Louvre.

(Enter Colbert.)

KING

Speak, sir—what have you come to tell me?

COLBERT

That the Cardinal just died, Sire.

KING

Dead!

(after a moment of silence looking fixedly at Mr. Colbert)

So you are Mr. Colbert?

COLBERT

Yes, Sire.

KING

The Keeper of His Eminence's secrets?

COLBERT

Of all.

KING

You are a financier, sir?

COLBERT

Yes, Sire.

KING

The Cardinal employed you as his steward?

COLBERT

Yes, Sire—I had the honor of being so employed and it was I that His Eminence charged to examine the accounts of the ministry.

KING

Ah! Ah! It's you who watch over Mr. Fouquet? And the result of that oversight?

COLBERT

There's deficit, Sire.

KING

Give me the summary—

COLBERT

Completely empty—no gold anywhere—Your Majesty sees that's simple.

KING

Be careful—you are brutally attacking Mr. Fouquet's administration—who is, I've heard say, a very clever man.

COLBERT

Yes, Sire, a very clever man.

KING

But if Mr. Fouquet is a clever man, and despite his cleverness money is lacking—who's at fault?

COLBERT

I don't accuse, Sire—I authenticate.

KING

If there's a deficit this year—so be it, but next year—

COLBERT

Next year is devoured, Sire, as short as the current year—

KING

Well—the year after then?

COLBERT

Like next year, four years are engaged in advance.

KING

There will be a loan.

COLBERT

There have already been three.

KING

Still—

COLBERT

May Your Majesty formulate his thought clearly and I will try to respond to it.

KING

You are right. Clarity above all, right?

COLBERT

Yes, Sire—God is God because He knew how to enlighten.

KING

Well—today the Cardinal died and I remain King—if I need money?

COLBERT

You won't have it.

KING

Then Mr. Fouquet, this clever man who just now offered me forty millions—won't be able to find me any money?

COLBERT

No, Sire.

KING

If things are as you say, Mr. Colbert, I am ruined before I reign.

COLBERT

You are indeed, Sire.

KING

Still, sir—the money is somewhere.

COLBERT

Yes, Sire—and even to begin I am bringing to Your Majesty an account of funds that the Cardinal didn't want to mention either in his will or in any deed whatever but which he confided to me.

KING

To you?

COLBERT

Yes, Sire.

KING

Above and beyond the forty millions in the will?

COLBERT

He knew you would refuse them.

KING

Who told him that?

COLBERT

I did, Sire.

KING

You? Ah, you judged me well, sir. And the sum you are bringing me—is it worth the trouble?

COLBERT

Thirteen million pounds—

KING

Thirteen million pounds. You say thirteen million pounds, Mr. Colbert?

COLBERT

Yes, Sire.

KING

That no one knows about?

COLBERT

No one.

KING

Which are in your hands?

COLBERT

In my hands.

KING

And that I can have?

COLBERT

In two hours.

KING

Why—where are they?

COLBERT

In the cellar of a house that the Cardinal owned in the city and that he willed to me by a special clause in his will.

KING

Then you know the Cardinal's will?

COLBERT

I have a duplicate.

(he shows it to the King)

KING

But here it's only a question of the house and no part of the money is mentioned?

COLBERT

Pardon, Sire—it's in my conscience.

KING

You are an honest man, sir.

COLBERT

That's not a virtue, Sire—it's a duty.

KING

Sir, what reward do you wish me to give you for this devotion and this probity?

COLBERT

Nothing—Sire.

KING

Not even the opportunity to serve me?

COLBERT

Your Majesty didn't furnish me this opportunity, yet I served him none the less.

KING

You will be the Minister of Finance, Mr. Colbert.

COLBERT

There's already a Minister, Sire.

KING

Exactly.

COLBERT

Sire, today, after the death of the Cardinal, the Finance Minister is the most powerful man in the realm.

KING

Ah, you think so.

COLBERT

He could crush me in a week, Sire. Your Majesty is giving me an authority for which power is indispensable.

KING

It appears you are not making money on me.

COLBERT

I have already had the honor to tell Your Majesty that in the time of the Cardinal, Mr. Fouquet was the second man in the realm, but now Cardinal Mazarin is dead—Mr. Fouquet is now first.

KING

Mr. Colbert—I warn you that although today I consent to your saying such things—but tomorrow I won't suffer it.

COLBERT

Then—from tomorrow I will be of no use to Your Majesty.

KING

Then what do you want? In your turn—speak clearly—

COLBERT

I want Your Majesty to give me aid in your work of the Ministry.

KING

Choose your colleagues—is that all?

COLBERT

Yes, Sire—I leave satisfied now.

KING

One moment, sir—

COLBERT

I am at the King's disposal.

KING

One question.

COLBERT

I'm prepared.

KING

Once I had in my service, as a lieutenant of the Musketeers a man who gave me his resignation.

COLBERT

At Blois—over a million that Your Majesty or rather the Cardinal refused to His Majesty Charles II.

KING

You know that?

COLBERT

I know everything the Cardinal knew.

KING

Well, could you tell me what has become of Mr. D'Artagnan?

COLBERT

Your Majesty is unaware that he contributed powerfully to the restoration of His Majesty Charles II?

KING

Yes—he must have taken service under my brother of England.

COLBERT

He refused some very fine offers they made him.

KING

Where is he?

COLBERT

I've not heard it said, that he left Great Britain.

KING

I need Mr. D'Artagnan, Mr. Colbert.

COLBERT

Wherever he may be, he will be found.

KING

That's fine—you may so, sir.

(Colbert leaves.)

KING

I will be very astonished if that man isn't in Mr. Fouquet's place within 3 months.

USHER

(entering)

Sire, a letter, coming from England by special messenger.

KING

Give it here—ah, it's on the subject of marriage of my brother, Philippe, with Miss Henriette of England.

(to usher)

Have the courier who brings this letter enter.

USHER

(at the door calling)

Mr. D'Artagnan!

(D'Artagnan enters.)

KING

Mr. D'Artagnan! At the moment that I asked for him, at the moment that I have need of him. Could this be what they call the luck of Kings?

(to D'Artagnan who has come in)

It's you who bring me this letter from England, sir?

D'ARTAGNAN

Yes, Sire—King Charles II, knowing I was going to France didn't think he could find a more faithful hand to deliver it to you.

KING

Sir—

D'ARTAGNAN

Sire!

KING

You know without doubt that the Cardinal is dead?

D'ARTAGNAN

No, Sire, but I'd begun to suspect it.

KING

You know, in consequence, that I am my own master?

D'ARTAGNAN

Sire, one is always one's own master when one wishes to be.

KING

You recall what you told me at Blois—the day you left my service?

D'ARTAGNAN

It was a long time ago, Sire, that I had the honor to have that conversation with Your Majesty.

KING

Well, if your memory is defective, as for me, I recall. You commenced by telling me, sir, that you had served my family for a long while and that you were worn out.

D'ARTAGNAN

It's true, Sire, I said that.

KING

Then later you admitted that this fatigue was a pretext and discontent was the real cause of your retreat.

D'ARTAGNAN

I was discontented, indeed, Sire—but this discontentment did not betray itself in any way that I know of—and I was a man of heart, I spoke openly before Your Majesty, I never even thought it in the presence of others.

KING

Don't excuse yourself and continue to listen to me. As you reproached me that you were discontent you received in reply a promise. I told you "Wait", right?

D'ARTAGNAN

Yes, Sire.

KING

In your turn, you replied to me "Wait? No—right away—now, or never!" Don't excuse yourself—that's quite natural—Only you had no charity toward your prince, Mr. D'Artagnan.

D'ARTAGNAN

Sire, charity for a King—from a poor soldier?

KING

Oh! You understand me, sir—you know quite well about charity—you know indeed I needed charity—You knew quite well I wasn't master—You knew quite well that I had the future in expectancy—All that counted for nothing—You answered me—"My leave—right away."

D'ARTAGNAN

(gnawing his mustache)

Again, that's true.

KING

You didn't flatter me when I was in distress, sir.

D'ARTAGNAN

(raising his head)

If I didn't flatter Your Majesty, neither did I betray him—I watched like a dog at the door of my King—knowing perfectly well they wouldn't throw me bread or a bone—and that poor as well, I had nothing to hope for except the discharge Your Majesty reproaches me for.

KING

You've reflected, since I presume?

D'ARTAGNAN

About what, Sire?

KING

Why about all I told you then, sir?

D'ARTAGNAN

Yes, Sire.

KING

And haven't you waited for an opportunity to withdraw your words?

D'ARTAGNAN

I don't understand very well what Your Majesty is doing me the honor of telling me.

KING

Huh?

D'ARTAGNAN

Would you excuse me, Sire, my mind has grown very lazy and my skull very thick with age; things only penetrate it with difficulty—It's true that once entered, they remain there.

KING

You are going to understand me. You told me at Blois that you weren't rich?

D'ARTAGNAN

I am now.

KING

That's not my concern. You have your money, not mine. That's not my concern.

D'ARTAGNAN

I don't understand yet very well.

KING

Let's dot the i's. Do you have 25,000 pounds a year fixed income?

D'ARTAGNAN

Why, Sire?

KING

Have you enough for 4 horses provided and furnished by me—and more in supplementary funds if you were to ask it, according to occasion and necessity—or would you prefer a fixed income of an additional 25,000 pounds? Look—answer, sir, or I will believe indeed that you no longer have the rapidity of judgment. I always appreciated in you.

D'ARTAGNAN

Sire, 50,000 pounds per year is a sum that appears sufficient to me to face many eventualities.

KING

Let's pass them to something more important.

D'ARTAGNAN

But, Sire, I had the honor of saying to Your Majesty—.

KING

That you wanted to rest—I know quite well—only—I don't want that—I am the master, I believe.

D'ARTAGNAN

Yes, Sire.

KING

Right! You were formerly in line to become Captain of Musketeers.

D'ARTAGNAN

I was lieutenant—and I had my order in blank—

KING

Well—here's your order—signed this time.

D'ARTAGNAN

Sire!

KING

You accept.

D'ARTAGNAN

Oh—yes—

KING

Then, sir—starting today you are going to enter into functions. The Company of Musketeers has become completely disorganized since your departure—the men are loafing and haunting the cabarets where they fight despite my edicts and those of my father. You will reorganize the service as rapidly as possible.

D'ARTAGNAN

Yes, Sire.

KING

You will never leave my person.

D'ARTAGNAN

Fine!

KING

And you will march with me into the army where you and your men will take up general quarters around my tent.

D'ARTAGNAN

Then, Sire, if it's to impose a service like this on me, Your Majesty, doesn't need to give me 25,000 pounds.

KING

And as for me—I intend for you to have a stately house, and keep open table—as my Captain of Musketeers— in short—as an important person.

D'ARTAGNAN

As for me, Sire, I don't like easy money, I want to earn it, Your Majesty, is offering me a lazy man's job that the first comer would take for 4,000 pounds.

KING

You are a clever Gascon, Mr. D'Artagnan, and you will extract the secret from my heart.

D'ARTAGNAN

Good! Your Majesty has a secret.

KING

Yes, sir—

D'ARTAGNAN

Then I accept the 25,000 pounds and even the fifty—; for I will keep that secret, and discretion has no price these days—does Your Majesty wish to speak now?

KING

Much later.

USHER

(announcing)

The Count de la Fère.

D'ARTAGNAN

Athos!

KING

Who are you calling, Athos?

D'ARTAGNAN

It's true, Sire, you don't know that under that name is one of the most valiant men of your realm and one of the most noble hearts on earth.

KING

Little matter, sir, under what name I know him, since I know him. Will you be happy to see him and announce to him yourself that you've been named Captain General of the Musketeers?

D'ARTAGNAN

Enchanted, Sire!

KING

(to Usher)

Show in the Count de la Fère.

ATHOS

(entering)

Sire.

KING

(to Athos)

Sir, didn't you see, on entering a man who calls himself one of your good friends.

ATHOS

Where the King is, Sire, I see only the King.

KING

Well—I permit you to see Mr. D'Artagnan my Captain General of Musketeers—and to embrace him.

D'ARTAGNAN

Dear Athos!

ATHOS

Friend, I congratulate you with all my heart and I especially congratulate His Majesty for having given you the reward that you've deserved for so long.

KING

Count, allow me to hope you've come to ask something of me.

ATHOS

I won't hide from Your Majesty that I came indeed to solicit—

KING

Well, de la Fère, let's see what I can do for you.

ATHOS

Sire, what I wish to obtain from Your Majesty concerns the Vicomte de Bragellone, my son—he's thinking of marrying—

KING

Ah! Well, I intend to find him a wife—

ATHOS

He's found her, Sire—and only seeks the assent of Your Majesty.

KING

It's only a question of signing a contract of marriage? Fine. What's his fiancée's name?

ATHOS

It's Miss de la Vallière de la Baume le Blanc—

KING

Ah, yes—I know—she was presented to me—she's one of the maids of honor designated to the service of the future Madame Henriette of England.

ATHOS

That's it! Exactly.

KING

She's rich?

ATHOS

Not precisely—15-20,000 pounds in dowry at least, Sire, but those in love are disinterested—as for myself, I put little stock in money.

KING

With 1,500 pounds of dowry, without a pension, a woman cannot deal with the court. We will supply it. I intend to do that for Bragellone. Let's pass from money to quality, she's indeed the daughter of the Marquis de la Vallière—that's fine, but we have this good Saint Remy who wastes the house a bit with a woman, I know, and you, Count, you cling strongly to your house?

ATHOS

As for me, Sire, I don't cling to anything except my devotion to Your Majesty.

KING

Count, you surprise me: You just addressed a request to me about marriage—and you don't seem to me to be making this demand with a good heart.

ATHOS

Well, Sire, that's true.

KING

Then I don't understand you: refuse.

ATHOS

No, Sire, I love Raoul with all my paternal love; he's taken with Miss de la Vallière, he's forging a paradise for the future; I'm not one of those who wish to destroy the illusions of youth.

KING

Let's se, Count—does she love him?

ATHOS

If Your Majesty prefers, I will tell him the truth; I don't believe much in the love of Miss de la Vallière. She takes pleasure in seeing the Court, of being in the service of the Court, of being in the service of Madame, hesitating, I fear, in her head, so that she could not have a fondness in her heart—So it will probably be a marriage such as Your Majesty some time sees at court—but Raoul wants it—so let it be then—

KING

You don't resemble those soft fathers who are the slaves of their children?

ATHOS

Sire, I have a will against evil doers, I don't against people with heart. Raoul is suffering—he feels pain—I don't wish to deprive Your Majesty of services he can render.

KING

I understand—

ATHOS

Then I have no need to tell Your Majesty my goal is to make these children or rather this child happy as fast as possible.

KING

And as for me, I want, as you do, the happiness of Mr. de Bragellone—I don't say he'll never marry Miss de la Vallière—but I don't want him to marry her before she's made a fortune—And she on her side, deserves my good graces, such that I mean to give her—in a word, Count, I want them to wait.

ATHOS

Sire, once more.

KING

Count—you came, you said to ask a favor of me?

ATHOS

Yes, surely.

KING

Well—grant me one—let's not speak of this anymore. It's possible, away from here I will make war. I have need of free gentlemen around me. I would hesitate to send under balls and canons a newly-married man—a father of a family—I would hesitate also—for Bragellone's sake to give a dowry, without an important reason to a young unknown girl—that would spread the seed of jealousy amongst my nobles. Is that all that you have to ask of me?

ATHOS

Absolutely all, Sire—and I take leave of Your Majesty—but should I warn Raoul?

KING

Spare yourself that concern; tell the Vicomte that I will speak to him—as for this evening, you will be at my gaming table?

ATHOS

I'm in traveling clothes, Sire—

KING

A day will come, I hope, when you won't leave me anymore. Above all, Count, the monarchy will be established in this manner—by offering a worthy hospitality to all men of your merit.

ATHOS

Sire, so long as King is great in the hearts of his subjects little matter the palace he occupies since he is adored in a temple.

(Athos goes to rejoin D'Artagnan who has remained at the back.)

KING

Come, the day is good! Thirteen millions in my cellars. Mr. Colbert holds the treasury; D'Artagnan the sword—I am truly King!

BLACKOUT

ACT I
SCENE 2

In the Forest of Fontainebleau—by the Royal Oak.

AURE

(entering and looking about)

Nobody! Come Athénaïs, come Louise!

LOUISE

(smiling)

Beautiful walk in these words of Fontainebleau! Nice plan we formed of passing the night without overseers and without escorts while our service as Ladies of Honor to Madame leaves us a little liberty. You remember, Montalais, the words of Chaverny and Chambard? The endless poplars of Blois? We exchanged many hopes there.

AURE

Alas.

LOUISE

Ah, merry Montalais, how you sigh, the words inspire you and you are almost reasonable this evening.

ATHÉNAÏS

Ladies, you ought not to regret Blois so much that you don't find yourself happy with us; a court's a place where men and women come to discuss matters that their mothers and tutors severely forbid, at court one speaks of these things under the privilege of the King and Queen—isn't that pleasant?

LOUISE

Oh—Athénaïs!

AURE

Athénaïs is frank tonight; let's profit by it.

ATHÉNAÏS

Yes, let's profit by it—for at this moment, they could tear the most intimate secrets of my heart from me.

AURE

Ah! If Mr. de Montespan were here!

ATHÉNAÏS

You think I love de Montespan? A well organized woman must be looked at by men, making them love, adore her even, and say once at least in her life "Heavens! It seems to me that if I hadn't been what I am—I would have detested that one less than the others."

LOUISE

(joining hands)

Then that's what you promise de Montespan?

ATHÉNAÏS

To him like anybody else.

AURE

Perfect! Athénaïs—you will go far—for it's with coquetting one is queen among women—when one hasn't received from God the precious faculty of building in one's heart and one's wit.

LOUISE

Oh, ladies, a loving heart is stronger than your coquetry! Love, the way I think of it, is constant sacrifice, absolute, total! It's the complete abrogation of two souls melting into one another—love is a shivering in the presence of the one loved—it's palpitating under the charm of his voice—it's to be annihilated by his glance—if I ever love, it will be with so much devotion and faith, that my greatest excuse will be in my love itself!

My life, my soul—I will give them—and if they cease to love me one day—well—I will die—at least God will help me—at least the Lord will take me in his mercy!

AURE

But, Louise, you are telling us that and you are not practicing it.

LOUISE

Me?

AURE

Yes, you—you've been adored for twelve years by Mr. Raoul de Bragellone—adored on both knees—! The poor lad is a victim of your virtue more than he would be of my coquetry or Athénaïs' pride.

LOUISE

What do you expect? Suppose I thought I loved—and I didn't.

AURE

What! You don't love?

LOUISE

If I've behaved differently than others do when they love it's because I don't love—it's because my time hasn't yet come.

ATHÉNAÏS

Then, decidedly, you don't love Mr. de Bragellone?

AURE

Perhaps! She really isn't sure yet. But in any case, listen, Athénaïs, if Mr. de Bragellone becomes free I give you a friend's advice.

ATHÉNAÏS

What is it?

AURE

It's to really look at him before deciding for Mr. de Montespan.

ATHÉNAÏS

Oh! If you are going there, my sweet, Mr. de Bragellone isn't the only one pleasing to look at—and, for example, Mr. de Saint-Aignan really has his price.

AURE

(to Louise)

Let's see—among all these gentlemen—which do you prefer?

LOUISE

I don't prefer any, ladies, I find them all equally fine—

ATHÉNAÏS

Then, in all this brilliant assembly, in the midst of this court, the first in the world—no one pleases you?

LOUISE

I didn't say that.

ATHÉNAÏS

Speak then—come on—share your ideal with us.

LOUISE

He's not an ideal.

AURE

Then 'he' exists?

LOUISE

Truly, ladies, I don't understand a thing. Like me, you have a heart, like me—you have eyes, and you speak of Mr. de Guiche, Mr. Saint-Aignan—what do I know—when the King is there—

AURE and ATHÉNAÏS

The King—

LOUISE

Yes, yes, the King! Is there someone who can be compared to him—? Ah, I know quite well he's not one of those that our eyes have the right to look on. Try then, if you like to avert my glances from this blazing sun. Choose among the Lords of the Court the one you imagine can make me forget this dream—this madness in my heart—but choose carefully so that my love will not involuntarily return to the King—the whole universe must guess my secret.

(on these words the King and Saint-Aignan enter—the King who has heard Louise gestures for Athénaïs and Aure to retire; they courtesy respectfully and do so without a word. Louise remains pensive then stands up looking for her friends.

Well—Montalais—Athénaïs—where are they? The King!

(she wants to withdraw)

KING

Stay put, miss.

LOUISE

Sire—

KING

Here's the rain—here the foliage is thick—but what's the matter with you? Are you cold, perhaps?

LOUISE

No, Sire.

KING

Yet you are trembling.

LOUISE

Sire, it's the fear my absence will be interpreted ill, when everyone is doubtless reunited.

KING

Miss, I would indeed suggest returning by carriage—but look—listen—tell me—if it is possible to attempt the least action at this moment?— Anyway there is no interpretation possible in your disfavor—aren't you with the King of France—that is to say with the first gentleman in the Kingdom?

LOUISE

(embarrassed)

Certainly, Sire.

KING

(aside)

Truly, she's charming!

LOUISE

Sire, here's the rain coming down and Your Majesty remains with your head uncovered.

KING

I beg you—let's only concern ourselves with you—miss.

LOUISE

Oh, me—I am used to running through the meadows and the woods of the Louvre—whatever the weather—as for my clothes, Your Majesty, they are no big thing to risk.

KING

Indeed, Miss, I've already noticed more than once that you keep pretty much to yourself and not your toilette—you are not a coquette and for me that's a great quality.

LOUISE

Sire, don't make me better than I am and say simply "You

cannot be a coquette."

KING

Why's that?

LOUISE

Why because I am not rich.

KING

Then you admit you like beautiful things?

LOUISE

It's kept away from me as if forbidden to me.

KING

And as for me, Miss—I don't find that you are on the footing you ought to be in my court. They certainly haven't spoken to me enough of your family's services—the fortune of your house was cruelly neglected by my uncle.

LOUISE

Sire, His Royal Highness Milord Duke of Orléans has always been perfectly good to Mr. de Saint-Remy—my step-father. The services were humble and we have been paid according to our works. Not everyone has the luck to find the opportunity to serve his King with distinction.

KING

Well, Miss, it's up to the King to rectify luck—and I take it upon myself joyously as quickly as possible on your behalf to right the wrongs of fortune.

LOUISE

They did all I desire, Sire, when they granted me the honor of becoming part of Madame's household.

KING

But, if you refuse for yourself, accept, at least for your family.

LOUISE

Sire, your intention is so generous it dazzles and frightens me, by doing for my family what your kindness urges you to do—Your Highness will make people envious of us—and create enemies.

KING

Ah—that's very disinterested language, Miss—but the rain is increasing—allow me—

(he places his hat over Louise's head)

LOUISE

Oh!

KING

What sad thought can come over your heart when I've made a rampart of mine over it?

LOUISE

A rampart of your heart, Sire?

KING

Yes, of my heart—for all that I see—all that I hear—penetrates it with esteem and admiration, and why should I be afraid to say it—of tenderness and—

LOUISE

(interrupting him)

Oh, Sire—there, I think the storm is calming and the rain stopping—and I'm going.

(clap of thunder)

(frightened)

Oh—Sire! Do you hear?

KING

(holding her in his arms)

Yes, you see clearly the storm hasn't passed.

LOUISE

It's a warning—it's the voice of God which threatens.

KING

Well, I accept the clap of thunder as a warning and even a

threat—if it renews with such force and equal violence, but if it's nothing—allow me to think that the storm is the storm and nothing else.

(the King raises his head to question heaven; the good weather returns)

The sky's clearing—see! Well, my Miss—are you threatening me again with celestial wrath? You are, you see, the divinity who makes the storm flee, the goddess who brings fine weather back.

LOUISE

Sire, doubtless they are looking for you—the Queen must be worried—and Madame, oh, Madame.

KING

Madame, you said?

LOUISE

Yes, Madame—Madame—

KING

Finish.

LOUISE

Oh, Sire—I don't dare.

KING

Oh, Miss—will you be one of those who think that Madame,

Madame the wife of my brother, has the right to be jealous of me?

LOUISE

Sire, it's not for me to penetrate Your Majesty's secrets.

KING

Oh—you believe it like the others do—

LOUISE

I think that Madame is jealous—yes.

KING

Miss—get this straight, Madame has no rights over me—I love her and I respect her as a brother ought to love and respect his sister.

LOUISE

Sire, they are coming.

KING

Well, Miss—let them come—who dares find anything amiss that I was keeping company with Miss de la Vallière?

LOUISE

Sire, mercy—they will find it strange that you remained so long here that you sacrificed yourself for me.

KING

I am only doing my duty as a gentleman and ill luck to whoever does not do his by criticizing the conduct of his King.

(Everyone enters.)

LOUISE

(terrified)

Madame.

MADAME

(to Vardes—pointing to the King and Louise)

The King with Miss de la Vallière—what's that mean, Mr. de Vardes?

DE VARDES

(low)

We're going to find out, Madame.

CURTAIN

ACT II
SCENE 3

The Governor's office at the Bastille.

D'ARTAGNAN

Mr. de Montlezun, governor of the Bastille?

LACKEY

He's making his afternoon rounds. Who shall I announce to him?

D'ARTAGNAN

The Chevalier d'Artagnan, Captain-General of the King's Musketeers.

(the lackey leaves)

My word since I have the title—might as well use it, since I probably won't have it as long as I've waited for it.

MONTLEZUN

(in the wings)

Mr. D'Artagnan—Captain General of the Musketeers of the King—? Mr. D'Artagnan takes the trouble of coming himself?

(Entering.)

D'ARTAGNAN

To visit an old friend—what's surprising in all that?

MONTLEZUN

But still, how does it happen that at the very moment I have the greatest need to see you, you arrive just in time?

D'ARTAGNAN

You know that's always the way I arrive. But so you won't think it's enchantment, I'm going to tell you what it's about.

MONTLEZUN

Sit down there.

D'ARTAGNAN

In returning to Planchet's I learned Mr. Montlezun did me the honor of coming to get news of me three times—once yesterday, twice today. So, I said to myself, "When the governor of the Bastille bothers himself to come to see a simple individual—for it's evident that you thought I was a simple individual—right?"—the situation must be grave. I said to myself, "I'm going to take a walk on foot all the way to the Bastille—that'll rest me from the horse."

MONTLEZUN

And you've come, admirable man!

D'ARTAGNAN

And I've come like you say.

MONTLEZUN

A thousand thanks for your courtesy, Chevalier.

D'ARTAGNAN

Say—my curiosity, do you remember that axiom—"To be curious sometimes injures others never oneself." I am listening to you. Speak.

MONTLEZUN

Well, it's true, I went by your place today for the third time. I thought to have a little imprisonment to do—and I returned to the Louvre in this hope: nope! The King had given a counter-order.

(sighing)

Ah, it's you who have a beautiful position, my dear Mr. D'Artagnan—Captain-General of the King's Musketeers.

D'ARTAGNAN

And what about you? Governor of the Bastille—the greatest person in the state of France.

MONTLEZUN

I know quite well there are folks who envy my position.

D'ARTAGNAN

You say that like a penitent, Damn! I'll change my perquisites against yours if you like.

MONTLEZUN

Don't speak to me of my perquisites. Chevalier—alas, you are breaking my heart.

D'ARTAGNAN

Come, draw your sword—spill it, Montlezun, spill it.

MONTLEZUN

It will take a while if I were to tell you all I have to tell you.

D'ARTAGNAN

At least start—if it's too long, I will act as if you were an attorney and I was a judge—I'll go to sleep.

MONTLEZUN

First—let me give an order.

(pulls a bell)

D'ARTAGNAN

Give it—

MONTLEZUN

(to a lackey who enters)

When the person I am expecting presents himself—you'll take him through the secret corridor and you will warn me.

LACKEY

Yes, governor.

MONTLEZUN

Immediately.

LACKEY

The very instant.

(He leaves.)

MONTLEZUN

(to D'Artagnan who is counting on his fingers)

What are you counting?

D'ARTAGNAN

I was calculating what you could make—in a good year; a bad year; dear Mr. Montlezun; I bet it exceeds 50,000 pounds.

MONTLEZUN

And when will it increase to sixty?

D'ARTAGNAN

You astonish me, Montlezun, you behave like a grieved man—but damn it, look at you! I'm going to escort you to a mirror—you will see that you are plump, flourishing, fat and round like a cheese—that you have eyes like burning coals, and without this villainous frown that you affect to furrow your face, you would have the air of a perfect apple. Add to all that, 60,000 pounds of perquisites—you just admitted—and compare my commission to yours.

MONTLEZUN

You are forgetting a detail, dear Mr. D'Artagnan. That you received from the King's hands your captaincy.

D'ARTAGNAN

Not for long—this very day!

MONTLEZUN

While, as for me, I bought mine from the governor of the Bastille.

D'ARTAGNAN

It's true—from Louviere and Trumblay and they weren't men to give it to you for nothing.

MONTLEZUN

75,000 pounds to each of them, dear Mr. D'Artagnan—more, three years of revenue as a bribe.

D'ARTAGNAN

That's exorbitant.

MONTLEZUN

That's not all.

D'ARTAGNAN

What else?

MONTLEZUN

Failure of a single payment of 50,000 pounds at maturity and these gentlemen retake their commission.

D'ARTAGNAN

But how—reduced to your own resources were you able to undertake such conditions? For you, too—you were a simple Musketeer.

MONTLEZUN

I found a lender.

D'ARTAGNAN

Who's that?

MONTLEZUN

One of your friends.

D'ARTAGNAN

Who is it?

MONTLEZUN

Mr. de Herblay—he offered to answer for me—

D'ARTAGNAN

Aramis! Truly, you stupefy me—Aramis co-signed for you?

MONTLEZUN

As a gallant man.

D'ARTAGNAN

And he kept his word?

MONTLEZUN

Every 31st of May before noon I've had my 50,000 to distribute to my crocodiles.

D'ARTAGNAN

Then you owe 150,000 pounds to Aramis?

MONTLEZUN

Eh! There's what I despair of, it's that I owe him only 100,000.

D'ARTAGNAN

I don't understand.

MONTLEZUN

For two years, he came on the 31st of May before noon—but here we are on the 31st of May at six in the evening—and he hasn't come yet—at least—

(he rings—then to lackey)

No one?

LACKEY

(entering)

No one.

MONTLEZUN

Go—! So that tomorrow, if, according to the terms of the contract, I haven't paid these gentlemen in the afternoon, they will retake their commission and 250,000 pounds will have been given for nothing, Mr. D'Artagnan, given for absolutely nothing.

D'ARTAGNAN

Now, that is irritating.

MONTLEZUN

Do you grasp now why I have a frown on my face?

D'ARTAGNAN

Yes, my word—

MONTLEZUN

Do you grasp that despite this cheese-like roundness, this apple freshness, that I've reached the point of fearing I'll have neither cheese nor one apple to eat.

D'ARTAGNAN

It's desolating.

MONTLEZUN

That's why I passed by your place once yesterday, twice today. You alone could relieve me of pain.

D'ARTAGNAN

How's that?

MONTLEZUN

Mr. Aramis d'Herblay was your friend.

D'ARTAGNAN

He still is.

MONTLEZUN

Tell me his address then?

D'ARTAGNAN

Ah. I don't know it.

MONTLEZUN

Then I am ruined.

D'ARTAGNAN

Where are you going?

MONTLEZUN

I'm going to throw myself—

D'ARTAGNAN

Not into the moats of the Bastille, I hope?

MONTLEZUN

No—at the king's feet.

D'ARTAGNAN

That might be almost the same thing! Do you have a word of honor, Montlezun?

MONTLEZUN

You know me?

D'ARTAGNAN

Yes, well, give me your word that you won't open your mouth to anyone and especially to Aramis of the advice I am going to give you.

MONTLEZUN

Not to anyone.

D'ARTAGNAN

You want to put your hand on him, right?

MONTLEZUN

Yes—

D'ARTAGNAN

Well, go find Mr. Fouquet.

MONTLEZUN

What's the connection?

D'ARTAGNAN

Aramis belongs to Fouquet, body and soul.

MONTLEZUN

You've opened my eyes.

D'ARTAGNAN

But—word of honor?

MONTLEZUN

Oh—sacred!

(rings, then to lackey who appears)

No one?

LACKEY

No one.

MONTLEZUN

Hitch up the horses to the carriage. I'll take you back, Mr. D'Artagnan.

D'ARTAGNAN

Good—so I can be seen in your carriage—famous way to keep a secret.

MONTLEZUN

You are right. I'm losing my head. But how will you go?

D'ARTAGNAN

By God—on foot—as I came. Consciousness of having rendered you a service will make the way seem short and the journey light.

MONTLEZUN

Ah yes—a service—you can boast of having rendered me a service.

D'ARTAGNAN

Good luck, Montlezun!

MONTLEZUN

Let me put you outside; without that they won't let you leave.

D'ARTAGNAN

Plague! And what will the King say tomorrow at his lever when he doesn't find the Captain-General of the Musketeers? It's true I have 24 hours leave.

MONTLEZUN

(escorting D'Artagnan out)

Let out Mr. D'Artagnan, the Captain-General of the Musketeers.

ANOTHER VOICE

(in the wings)

Let out Mr. D'Artagnan—Captain-General of the Musketeers.

ANOTHER VOICE

(still further off)

Order of the governor.

(Meanwhile Aramis enters through a secret door.)

ARAMIS

(to himself)

D'Artagnan—Captain-General of the Musketeers, has he then joined the King's partisans? The Devil!

MONTLEZUN

Are the horses on the carriage?

LACKEY

Yes, governor.

MONTLEZUN

(turning to take his hat)

I'm ready.

ARAMIS

(seated in an armchair)

Are you leaving, governor?

MONTLEZUN

Mr. d'Herblay! Where'd you come from?

ARAMIS

I came by way of the corridor I usually enter by.

MONTLEZUN

Ah, my god, I'm going to be ill.

ARAMIS

From fear? My presence produces that result?

MONTLEZUN

No, sir—from joy.

ARAMIS

Isn't today the 31st of May?

MONTLEZUN

Ah, I hadn't forgotten.

ARAMIS

Weren't you expecting me?

MONTLEZUN

Actually, I was no longer expecting you.

ARAMIS

It's that tomorrow you owe your term—before noon; there's no time to lose.

MONTLEZUN

You are the most faithful man of your word.

ARAMIS

Ah, indeed! Tell me how are your affairs at the Bastille?

MONTLEZUN

(makes a spitting sound)

ARAMIS

Do the prisoners pay?

MONTLEZUN

Stingy.

ARAMIS

The devil—could we have made a bad investment?

MONTLEZUN

Cardinal Mazarin wasn't tough enough.

ARAMIS

Yes—you need our old Cardinal.

MONTLEZUN

Ah! Under that one everything went well—the brother of his Gray Eminence made his fortune at it.

ARAMIS

Things will improve, believe me, my dear governor—a young king is much more valuable than an old Cardinal—if old age has its grudges, its fears, its prudence, youth has its rages, its passions, its suspicions. Have you paid your three year payment to Louviere and Trumblay?

MONTLEZUN

Ah, my God, yes—

ARAMIS

So that all that remains to give them is the 50,000 pounds I'm bringing.

MONTLEZUN

Yes—only that.

ARAMIS

But no savings?

MONTLEZUN

Ah, Chevalier!

ARAMIS

How many prisoners have you?

MONTLEZUN

Sixteen.

ARAMIS

Why that seems to me to be a round enough figure.

MONTLEZUN

In the time of the other Cardinal there would have been almost 200, there were princes of the blood—and from princes of the blood, egad—the governor had 50,000 pounds a year.

ARAMIS

So that—today—no princes of the blood?

MONTLEZUN

No, thank God—that is to say unfortunately.

ARAMIS

And from a Marshall of France, how much does the governor have?

MONTLEZUN

Thirty-six pounds.

ARAMIS

And no more Marshals of France than Princes of the blood?

MONTLEZUN

Alas, no—it's true that Lieutenant Generals and Brigadiers are twenty-four pounds and I've got two.

ARAMIS

Ha! Ha!

MONTLEZUN

After that, there are parliamentary councilors—who bring fifteen pounds—

ARAMIS

And you have—

MONTLEZUN

Four—

ARAMIS

I didn't know that councilors bring such a good revenue.

MONTLEZUN

Yes, but from fifteen pounds, I fall to ten.

ARAMIS

To ten?

MONTLEZUN

Ten for an ordinary judge—for an attorney or a priest I get seven.

ARAMIS

Good business.

MONTLEZUN

Bad business—on the contrary.

ARAMIS

Why's that?

MONTLEZUN

Because—I have, despite myself, mercy for them and I treat them like councilors.

ARAMIS

But then, the meanest prisoners—how much for them?

MONTLEZUN

Three pounds per day—the small bourgeois—the ushers and clerks—the poets.

ARAMIS

Ah! The three pound per day prisoners must be very wretched.

MONTLEZUN

On the contrary—they think they are the kings of creation.

ARAMIS

Explain that to me.

MONTLEZUN

You grasp that I cannot be of use to the Lieutenant Generals, the Marshals of France and Princes of the blood—since I don't have them.

ARAMIS

Logical.

MONTLEZUN

While I serve the three-pound prisoners, the remains of the twenty-four pounds—to fifteen and fifteen: so that they nibble on dishes they've only seen in dreams. Ah—those there bless me—they regret the prison when they leave it—would you believe—

ARAMIS

What?

MONTLEZUN

Certain prisoners—hardly released get themselves re-incarcerated to get the Bastille's cuisine—you don't believe it—

ARAMIS

I admit it.

MONTLEZUN

We have names brought in two or three times in the space of two years.

ARAMIS

I'll have to see that to believe it.

MONTLEZUN

They can show you—

ARAMIS

Where?

MONTLEZUN

On the registers.

ARAMIS

I thought you were forbidden to communicate the register to strangers.

MONTLEZUN

It's true—but you are not a stranger.

ARAMIS

That's right; show me that my dear Mr. de Montlezun.

MONTLEZUN

Choose a letter at random.

ARAMIS

Whatever you like: The letter M for instance.

MONTLEZUN

The letter M—so be it—here, I open—M—Martiner January 1659, Martiner, June 1660; Martiner, March 1661—pamphlets, libels against Mazarin, etc., etc." You understand it was only a pretext; he wasn't imprisoned for the libels; the wise guy denounced himself so he'd be sent back to eat my cuisine.

ARAMIS

And his neighbor? Here the name I saw there—Marchiali.

MONTLEZUN

Hush!

ARAMIS

Is he also a poet?

MONTLEZUN

Hush!

ARAMIS

Why hush?

MONTLEZUN

I thought you'd already heard of this Marchiali.

ARAMIS

No—this is the first time I've heard his name mentioned.

MONTLEZUN

It's possible; I would have spoken to you without mentioning his name.

ARAMIS

And his crime is so great?

MONTLEZUN

Unpardonable!

ARAMIS

He murdered?

MONTLEZUN

Bah!

ARAMIS

Arsonist—

MONTLEZUN

That would be nothing.

ARAMIS

Slandered?

MONTLEZUN

No—it's that he—

ARAMIS

He—?

MONTLEZUN

He allows himself to resemble the King.

ARAMIS

(to himself)

Finally, I'"m there.

(aloud)

Indeed, dear Mr. Montlezun—you may have said a few words to me about it last year—but in the crime appears to me so slight—

MONTLEZUN

Slight?

ARAMIS

Or rather so involuntary. Anyway, I'd forgotten him, because I told myself this resemblance was probably imaginary.

MONTLEZUN

Ah! Imaginary—! Whoever sees the prisoner—

ARAMIS

Whoever sees the prisoner?

MONTLEZUN

(lowering his voice)

—Sees the King.

ARAMIS

(shaking his head)

I think that's all simply a figment of your imagination, my dear governor—

MONTLEZUN

No, on my oath—! I know indeed that there are resemblances and resemblances—but this one is striking and if you were to see him.

ARAMIS

Well?

MONTLEZUN

You would yourself agree. Unfortunately, it's forbidden to introduce strangers into the prisoner's rooms.

ARAMIS

You said just now I was not a stranger.

MONTLEZUN

To me, yes—but not to the turnkey, who would see you enter the room.

ARAMIS

Indeed—there's a misfortune—as you say—I confess I am not anxious but I would really give something to see this—what do you call him?

MONTLEZUN

Marchiali.

ARAMIS

Marchiali.

MONTLEZUN

Hold on!

ARAMIS

What?

MONTLEZUN

An idea.

ARAMIS

You are invention personified.

MONTLEZUN

The fact is I'd throw myself in the fire to be agreeable to you.

ARAMIS

I would never demand that of you—don't worry—you were saying?

MONTLEZUN

I was saying that, if you cannot go into a prisoner's room, no rule forbids me from having a prisoner come to my room.

ARAMIS

Doubtless you could make him come here.

MONTLEZUN

Marchiali.

(with urgency)

Tell the chief of the jailers to have the 2nd Berthandière come to me.

ARAMIS

My dear governor, excuse me, but you speak a language that requires a certain apprenticeship.

MONTLEZUN

That's true, pardon—the 2nd Berthandière, you see, means whoever is occupying the second floor of the Towers of la Berthandière. Once in the Bastille—you no longer have a name—you become a number.

ARAMIS

I'm going to see some wretch—dying—almost a shade, some ghost?

MONTLEZUN

Not at all: A young man—a strapping lad—firm as the Pont Neuf.

ARAMIS

And how much is this one?

MONTLEZUN

He's a fifteen pounder.

ARAMIS

Ah! Ah! A fifteen pounder! And why such magnificence?

MONTLEZUN

That's where you see the King's bounty shine.

ARAMIS

The King's?

MONTLEZUN

I mean that of the Cardinal, "This wretch," said Marazin, "is destined to remain in prison forever."

ARAMIS

Why forever—?

MONTLEZUN

It seems to me that the crime, being eternal—the punishment must be eternal also.

ARAMIS

Eternal.

MONTLEZUN

Doubtless, for without having the good fortune to catch small pox—which isn't likely in the Bastille, since the air here is excellent—

ARAMIS

So this wretch must suffer without respite—without end?

MONTLEZUN

Suffer—at fifteen pounds a day one doesn't suffer!

ARAMIS

Hush—I hear a step.

MONTLEZUN

It's him they are bringing—

(to Aramis who rises and removes his hat)

Well—what are you doing?

ARAMIS

That's right.

(the jailers enter with Marchiali)

(to himself)

I'm giving myself away.

(looking attentively at Marchiali)

My God! My God!

MONTLEZUN

Leave me alone with the prisoner—I have some questions to put to him.

(jailers leave. To Marchiali)

It's a long while since I've seen you, sir.

MARCHIALI

It's true.

MONTLEZUN

You look fine. It seems to me you are well.

MARCHIALI

Very well, sir.

MONTLEZUN

(to Aramis)

What do you say to that?

ARAMIS

Incredible—can I speak to him? Put some questions to him?

MONTLEZUN

No doubt.

ARAMIS

You are not bored—sir?

MARCHIALI

Never.

ARAMIS

(to Montlezun)

Can I ask him if he knows why he is here?

MONTLEZUN

You heard, Marchiali; the gentleman charges me to ask you if you know the reason for your detention?

MARCHIALI

No, sir—I don't know it.

ARAMIS

Impossible! If you knew the cause of your detention, you would be furious.

MARCHIALI

I was at first.

ARAMIS

Why aren't you any longer?

MARCHIALI

Because I considered.

ARAMIS

What?

MARCHIALI

I considered that—having committed no crime God couldn't punish me.

ARAMIS

To hear you, sir, to see your resignation, one would be tempted to believe that you love prison.

MARCHIALI

I bear it.

ARAMIS

In the certitude of being free some day?

MARCHIALI

I don't have certitude—I have hope—that's all—only each day this hope diminishes.

ARAMIS

But anyway—why won't you be free again—since you were once—?

MARCHIALI

It's precisely because I was once free that I despair of becoming so again. Why would they have imprisoned me if they'd had the intention of making me free later on?

MONTLEZUN

(who listens—as he writes)

You see—logical—

ARAMIS

How old are you?

MARCHIALI

I don't know.

ARAMIS

What name did you bear formerly?

MARCHIALI

I've forgotten it.

ARAMIS

You often recall your relatives?

MARCHIALI

I never knew them.

ARAMIS

But those who raised you?

MARCHIALI

They never called me their son.

ARAMIS

Did you love someone before coming here?

MARCHIALI

I loved my air, my flowers, my birds.

ARAMIS

Is that all?

MARCHIALI

I also loved my valet.

ARAMIS

You regret this nurse and valet much?

MARCHIALI

I cried a lot when they died.

ARAMIS

Did they die after you came here?

MARCHIALI

They died the morning of the day they carried me off.

ARAMIS

Both—the same day?

MARCHIALI

Both—the same day.

ARAMIS

And how did they carry you off?

MARCHIALI

A man came to fetch me—made me get in a locked carriage and brought me here.

ARAMIS

Would you recognize this man?

MARCHIALI

He had a mask.

MONTLEZUN

(to Aramis)

Isn't this story very extraordinary?

ARAMIS

It couldn't be more so.

MONTLEZUN

But what's still more extraordinary is that he's never spoken to anyone but you.

ARAMIS

Perhaps that's because you've never questioned him.

MONTLEZUN

It's possible. I am not curious.

ARAMIS

(to Marchiali)

Don't you recall having been visited by some stranger or some foreigner?

MARCHIALI

Three times a lady stopped a carriage at the gate and entered covered with a veil—which she did not raise when we were alone.

ARAMIS

You remember this lady?

MARCHIALI

Yes.

ARAMIS

What did she say to you?

MARCHIALI

She asked me what you are asking of me—if I was happy—and if I was bored.

ARAMIS

And when she came or left?

MARCHIALI

She embraced me—she pressed me against her heart and held me in her arms.

ARAMIS

And you recall the features of her face?

MARCHIALI

Yes.

ARAMIS

And you would recognize her if chance brought her to you or led you to her?

MARCHIALI

I would recognize her.

MONTLEZUN

(to Aramis)

Well—have you seen all you wanted to see?

ARAMIS

Everything.

MONTLEZUN

Did I exaggerate the resemblance?

ARAMIS

You understated the reality.

MONTLEZUN

Next time will you believe me?

ARAMIS

On your word.

(to Marchiali)

Now, sir, it remains for the governor and I to apologize for having disturbed you.

MONTLEZUN

Come now!

MARCHIALI

You haven't disturbed me, sir—and it pleased me greatly to walk across the courtyard. The air is so nice.

(he sighs)

MONTLEZUN

(going to open the door)

Take the prisoner back.

(the jailers enter and retake Marchiali who bows. Montlezun lightly returns his bow—Aramis on the contrary bows deeply)

MONTLEZUN

Well—what do you say to all that?

ARAMIS

I say it's extraordinary and incomprehensible! Now, my dear governor let's return to our little arrangements. Here's your last 50,000 pounds.

MONTLEZUN

A hundred thanks, Mr. d'Herblay. What terms do you give me for reimbursement? Fix it yourself.

ARAMIS

Eh, my God—don't take any term; just a recognition pure and simple of 150,000 pounds.

MONTLEZUN

On demand.

ARAMIS

At my will; but you understand I will only want it when you do.

MONTLEZUN

(writing)

I've given you two receipts.

ARAMIS

Here they are. I am tearing them up.

(he reads over Montlezun's shoulder)

MONTLEZUN

Good enough? Read!

ARAMIS

Come on! Read after you!

(he puts the obligation in his pocket—aside)

It was indispensable to have the governor of the Bastille as a debtor and to oblige him.

(aloud)

By the way—you must have a young prisoner here—I was forgetting that poor devil.

MONTLEZUN

A young prisoner!

ARAMIS

Yes, around the age of Marchiali.

MONTLEZUN

You call him?

ARAMIS

Seldon.

MONTLEZUN

Ah, yes, a poet. He's here for having composed two poems against I don't know who—

ARAMIS

He's been recommended to me; you won't wish me ill—if one day, I obtain his pardon and carry him off from you?

MONTLEZUN

A three pounder? Ah, by God, you are indeed the master. That sort, I told you, cost me more than they bring to me.

ARAMIS

Anyway, I don't know if I will succeed.

MONTLEZUN

Oh—you have a long arm and a large hand. Goodbye!

ARAMIS

Goodbye, my dear governor—

(aside)

Go! Madame de Chevreuse told me the truth. This won't happen to him very often; Marchiali is the brother of the King.

CURTAIN

ACT II
SCENE 4

A room in the Palace of Fontainebleau.

ARAMIS

So, my dear Superintendent—you are going to present me to the King?

FOUQUET

The audience I've asked His Majesty for this morning has no other object—but where is Porthos? For I intend to present him to the King as well. It was, I believe, his dream to be presented—and since he's one of us—but I don't see him.

ARAMIS

He's finishing his toilette. The toilette of Porthos is quite an affair.

FOUQUET

Aramis! Porthos! With friends like that, what couldn't we undertake? Ah, if we had D'Artagnan and Athos with us.

ARAMIS

Yes, we could begin all over again the great battles of former times—but we lack D'Artagnan—he's for the King—as for Athos—unusual circumstances will perhaps give us his son.

FOUQUET

What do you mean?

ARAMIS

Here it is: As you know, Athos has asked the King for the hand of Miss de la Vallière on behalf of the Vicomte de Bragellone. The king refused his consent to this marriage or rather postponed it—This isn't all—some time ago, the King gave Mr. de Bragellone a message for His Majesty Charles II. Mr. de Bragellone left for England—this voyage coupled with certain attentions the King seems to have for la Vallière is significant. Then, if Athos and his son begin to suspect something, who knows what will become of their sentiments of fidelity and devotion to the King? By the way, have you sent Miss de la Vallière the letter I advised you to write to her?

FOUQUET

To Miss de la Vallière?

ARAMIS

Yes—did you declare yourself her zealous servant—what shall I say—her worshipper?

FOUQUET

Right! I remember now you advised me on this subject—but

really, were you serious?

ARAMIS

Very serious.

FOUQUET

What advantage do you see in my occupying myself with Miss de la Vallière?

ARAMIS

What advantage? A very great one! Believe me—make yourself a friend of Miss de la Vallière; for you—it's a very easy thing—your signature at the bottom of a tender letter—worth a million.

FOUQUET

Money! Again!

ARAMIS

Are you going to be worried for a million—more or less?

FOUQUET

But think how it pinches me there! I became powerful through money and it's with money they are trying to beat me down. If you knew what it cost me to procure the most recent sums I poured into the King's treasury!

ARAMIS

It's necessary now that you resist to the very end. Again, some sacrifices—and you will be rewarded beyond your most mad or demanding dreams.

FOUQUET

Indeed, my dear Mr. d'Herblay, your confidence frightens me even more than the hate of my enemies!

ARAMIS

Bah!

FOUQUET

Ah, indeed! Who are you?

ARAMIS

You know me—it seems to me?

FOUQUET

My mistake—rather—what do you want?

ARAMIS

What do I want? I want a King on the throne of France who will be devoted to Mr. Fouquet and I want Mr. Fouquet to be devoted to me.

FOUQUET

Oh, as for belonging to you—I indeed belong to you, but believe me my dear d'Herblay—you are deluding yourself.

ARAMIS

In what?

FOUQUET

The King will never be devoted to me.

ARAMIS

I never said the King would be devoted to you.

FOUQUET

Why, on the contrary, you just said it.

ARAMIS

I never said the King—I said a king.

FOUQUET

Isn't that the same thing?

ARAMIS

It's very different.

FOUQUET

I don't get it.

ARAMIS

Suppose that the King were a man other than Louis XIV.

FOUQUET

Another man?

ARAMIS

Yes, who owed everything to you.

FOUQUET

Impossible.

ARAMIS

Even his throne.

FOUQUET

Oh—you are mad! There is no other man than King Louis XIV who could sit on the throne of France. I don't see a single one.

ARAMIS

As for me, I see one!

FOUQUET

At least it cannot be Monsieur, the King's brother—why Monsieur—

ARAMIS

It's not Monsieur.

FOUQUET

Then how would you want a prince who wouldn't be of the blood—how would you want a prince who would have no right?

ARAMIS

(interrupting him)

Don't worry—my King—mine—or rather your king—will be all that he ought to be—

FOUQUET

Take care, take care, Aramis! You're giving me the shivers, you're giving me vertigo.

ARAMIS

You get the shivers and vertigo rather easily—

FOUQUET

One more time, you terrify me—you are laughing.

ARAMIS

The day will come when you'll laugh like me—now I must be the only one to laugh.

FOUQUET

But explain yourself—!

ARAMIS

Much later—while waiting, fear nothing. Write your letter and get it to a la Vallière very quickly—do you have someone trusty for that?

FOUQUET

I have Toby, my confidential valet.

(some lords enter)

ARAMIS

Fine.

USHER

The King.

FOUQUET

The King! And Porthos—where is Porthos?

D'ARTAGNAN

(entering)

He's here—I'll bring him to you.

ARAMIS

(shaking his hand)

D'Artagnan.

PORTHOS

(entering breathless)

Excuse me! It seems that I am late—but you understand—my toilette!

ARAMIS

You are handsome like the sun.

KING

(entering)

(to Fouquet)

Ah, it's you, Mr. Fouquet, be welcome.

FOUQUET

Your Majesty overwhelms me—and since he is so good as to allow me to remind him of our audience he promised me.

KING

Yes, for two of your friends, I recall.

FOUQUET

Perhaps the time is ill chosen, Sire.

KING

Not at all! Not at all! Where are your friends?

FOUQUET

Here, Sire!

KING

Let them approach.

(Aramis approaches—bows and waits. Porthos comes behind him)

FOUQUET

(presenting Aramis)

Mr. d'Herblay, Sire!

KING

You wanted to be presented to me, sir?

ARAMIS

I would never have had the ambition for such an honor if I had not been encouraged by my protector, Mr. Fouquet.

(aside, watching the King, while the King goes to Porthos)

That's it, it's impossible to doubt it.

FOUQUET

(presenting Porthos)

Monsieur, the Baron du Vallon—

PORTHOS

(low to Fouquet)

De Bracieux de Pierrefonds!

FOUQUET

I would have requested the honor of presenting him long ago, but some men resemble the stars, they don't go except with the company of their friends—they never separate. That's why I am lucky to find the right moment to present Mr. du Vallon and Mr. d'Herblay to you—the moment when Mr. D'Artagnan is close to Your Majesty.

KING

(looking at D'Artagnan)

These gentlemen are your friends?

D'ARTAGNAN

Yes, Sire!

(taking their hands)

My companions, as Musketeers, Mr. d'Herblay and Mr. du Vallon who, with Mr. de la Fère and myself for 20 years formed that quartet of which much was said under the late King and during the Regency.

KING

Well, gentlemen what can I do for you? I love to reward the servants of my father the King.

PORTHOS

Sire—Sire—Sire.

KING

(to Aramis)

Let's see Mr. d'Herblay.

ARAMIS

Sire, nothing remains for me to desire, nothing to ask, now that I've had the honor to be presented to Your Majesty.

(aside)

And to confirm this perfect resemblance to Marchiali.

KING

(to Porthos)

And you, Mr. du Vallon?

D'ARTAGNAN

Sire, this brave gentleman is dumbstruck by the dignity of your person. He would brave the fire of 1,000 enemies but cannot sustain your glance—but I know what he thinks, and as for me, more accustomed to gaze at the sun than he, I am going to tell you his thoughts—Sire—he desires nothing wants nothing—except to contemplate Your Majesty this evening.

KING

You with me, gentlemen. Mr. Fouquet, you, too.

ALL

Sire.

PORTHOS

(to D'Artagnan)

You'll place yourself near me at table, D'Artagnan.

D'ARTAGNAN

Yes, my friend.

PORTHOS

By the way—does the King like to eat a lot?

D'ARTAGNAN

That's flatters him, dear Porthos—for he possesses a royal appetite.

PORTHOS

You enchant me—I'll be very hungry tonight.

(The King accompanied by Fouquet passes before the groups of gentlemen who entered with him or followed him.)

ARAMIS

(to D'Artagnan)

This dear D'Artagnan! Do you know you are a unique man to praise your friends.

D'ARTAGNAN

My friends—you lean on that word in a singular manner.

ARAMIS

You still love me, my dear D'Artagnan?

D'ARTAGNAN

Surely.

ARAMIS

Well then, let's talk as in the good old days.

D'ARTAGNAN

I'm listening.

ARAMIS

Would you like to become Marshall of France, Duke, Peer, have a million?

D'ARTAGNAN

To obtain all that, what must be done—let's see?

ARAMIS

Be Mr. Fouquet's man, my friend.

D'ARTAGNAN

Impossible—I am the King's man—

ARAMIS

Not exclusively?

D'ARTAGNAN

There's only one D'Artagnan.

ARAMIS

But you have ambition, great heart that you are?

D'ARTAGNAN

Yes.

ARAMIS

Well?

D'ARTAGNAN

I want to be Marshall: the King will name me Marshall—I desire to be Duke and Peer—the King will make all that. Isn't the King the Master?

ARAMIS

No one contests that. But Louis XIII was the master under Richelieu.

D'ARTAGNAN

Yes, but Louis XIII didn't have D'Artagnan as his Captain-General of the Musketeers.

ARAMIS

Around the King, there are lots of stumbling blocks—

D'ARTAGNAN

Look, Aramis, I see everyone here thinks of himself and no one of this young Prince—I will support myself by supporting him.

ARAMIS

Fine—and ingratitude.

D'ARTAGNAN

Only the weak fear it.

ARAMIS

But if the King no longer needs you?

D'ARTAGNAN

On the contrary, my friend, in a short while from now he will have more need of me than ever—if another Vendome, a new Condé have to be arrested—who will arrest them?

(slapping his sword)

This one!

ARAMIS

You're right. Your hand, D'Artagnan.

D'ARTAGNAN

Here it is.

ARAMIS

I shake it with all my heart, for it's an inflexible hand—but honest to his friends and his enemies.

USHER

The table of the King.

ARAMIS

God protect you—Mr. Captain-General of the Musketeers.

D'ARTAGNAN

God protect you—Mr. Chevalier d'Herblay—

ARAMIS

(aside)

Come, D'Artagnan is not for us—but happily Athos remains for us—and Marchiali!

D'ARTAGNAN

There the situation is plainly stated.

KING

Gentlemen, take places—hats, gentlemen!

(everyone puts on his hat—the King alone remains uncovered)

PORTHOS

Why hats?

D'ARTAGNAN

That's the rule—at table, the King alone remains uncovered.

PORTHOS

(to D'Artagnan)

It seems to me, you can go to it, and that His Majesty encourages it?

D'ARTAGNAN

By Jove! Only—manage things so that if by chance the King speaks to you, he won't find you with your mouth full.

PORTHOS

Why?

D'ARTAGNAN

Because that would be disgraceful.

PORTHOS

The best way then—is not to dine at all; still, I'm hungry and all these delicious odors, delight at once my appetite and sense of smell.

D'ARTAGNAN

Don't advise yourself not to eat; you will make the King angry—the King doesn't like it that you be picky at dinner.

PORTHOS

But how to avoid having a full mouth when one is eating?

D'ARTAGNAN

It's simply a question of swallowing when the King addresses you.

PORTHOS

Oh—if it's only a question of swallowing.

KING

Mr. du Vallon.

PORTHOS

(swallowing)

Sire?

KING

Let someone pass the slices of lamb to Mr. du Vallon. Do you like dark meat, Mr. du Vallon?

PORTHOS

Sire, I like all.

D'ARTAGNAN

(whispering to him)

All that Your Majesty sends me.

PORTHOS

(repeating)

All that Your Majesty sends me.

(he slides a quarter of lamb on his plate)

KING

Well?

PORTHOS

Exquisite, Sire.

KING

Do they also have fine lambs in your province, Mr. du Vallon?

PORTHOS

Sire, I think that, in my province, as everywhere, the best first go to the King, but then I don't eat lamb in the same way as Your Majesty.

KING

And how do you eat it?

PORTHOS

Ordinarily, Sire, I can accommodate a lamb in its entirety.

KING

Ha! Ha! In its entirety.

PORTHOS

Yes, Sire.

KING

And in what manner?

PORTHOS

Like this—my cook—this character is a German, Sire—my cook crams the lamb in question with little sausages which he gets from a town in Alsace called Strasbourg, meatballs, he gets from Troyes, truffles and larks from Pithiviers, then he bones the lamb as he would poultry leaving the skin from which he's carefully removed the wool and which makes a brown crust around the body—with the result that when it's cut into nice slices from inside a gravy emerges that is both agreeable to the eye and exquisite to the palate.

KING

And you eat it?

PORTHOS

In its entirety, yes, Sire.

KING

Pass these partridges to Mr. du Vallon—he's an amateur; Mr. du Vallon, I shall never forget your lamb—and it's not too fat?

PORTHOS

No, Sire, the fat falls off at the same time as the gravy—it' floats off and then my squire removes it with a gold ladle which I had made just for this.

KING

You have a fine appetite and you make a fine table companion, Mr. du Vallon.

PORTHOS

Ah, by my word, Sire, if Your Majesty ever comes to Pierrefords, we shall each eat our lamb for you show me you have on your part, a nice appetite.

D'ARTAGNAN

(low to Porthos)

Porthos! Porthos!

PORTHOS

Well—what?

D'ARTAGNAN

Nothing, my friend.

KING

Will you taste these creams, Mr. du Vallon?

PORTHOS

Sire, Your Majesty, treats me very well though I didn't tell him the truth in its entirety.

KING

Speak, Mr. du Vallon, speak—

PORTHOS

Well, Sire, in making sweets, I only know pates and yet they have to be very solid—all these mousses inflate my stomach and fill a place that is very precious for me to be so ill occupied.

KING

(pointing to Porthos and signing)

Ah, gentlemen, look and admire! There's a true model of gastronomy—thus ate our fathers who knew how to eat—we no longer eat, we peck at our food. Give some of my wine to Mr.

du Vallon.

D'ARTAGNAN

My friend the King is doing you the greatest honor he can do you—he's sending you his wine.

PORTHOS

And as for me, I only receive it to drink the health of the King.

(rising)

KING

(to the guests who wait)

Come gentlemen, I accept the toast.

Porthos, D'Artagnan, Aramis, Fouquet raise glasses to the King.)

D'ARTAGNAN

Porthos if you can only swallow the half of this boar's head. I will see you duke and peer within the year.

PORTHOS

Now, I'll set myself to work for it.

KING

(in a low voice)

Gentlemen, it's impossible that a gentlemen who dines so well and with such fine teeth not be the most honest man in my kingdom.

D'ARTAGNAN

You hear, Porthos?

PORTHOS

Yes, I think I have a little favor.

D'ARTAGNAN

A little favor—you are sailing before the wind, my friend.

KING

Mr. Fouquet!

FOUQUET

Sire!

KING

Mr. du Vallon by inviting me just now so graciously to come share a lamb with him at Pierrefords, awakened in me a desire I've always had.

FOUQUET

What's that, Sire?

KING

To receive an invitation to you next party at Vaux.

FOUQUET

For my next party?

KING

They say that every month you give magnificent parties? Why have you never spoken to me of them?

FOUQUET

Sire, how could I hope that Your Majesty would descend from the high regions where he lives to the point of honoring my dwelling with His Royal presence?

PORTHOS

(to D'Artagnan)

I'm at the boars head.

D'ARTAGNAN

Well—attack!

KING

Excuses, Mr. Fouquet, excuses!

FOUQUET

I never spoke to His Majesty of my parties because I feared a refusal.

KING

And what made you fear this refusal?

FOUQUET

The boundless desire I had to see the King accept.

KING

Well, Mr. Fouquet, I intend to give public evidence of my favor—I not only accept an invitation—I invite myself.

FOUQUET

Thanks, my King.

KING

They tell marvels of your Château at Vaux. It must make you proud, Mr. Fouquet that the King is jealous of you?

FOUQUET

Proud and happy, Sire, since the day when the King is jealous of my Château, I will have something worthy to offer him.

KING

Well—Mr. Fouquet, prepare your party—and open all the doors of your Château.

(shakes Mr. Fouquet's hand)

PORTHOS

Say, D'Artagnan.

D'ARTAGNAN

What?

PORTHOS

It seems to me that His Majesty is no longer paying attention to me?

D'ARTAGNAN

What do you want, my friend, *sic transit gloria mundi*?

PORTHOS

Then I shall continue for myself alone.

FOUQUET

(to Aramis)

My dear d'Herblay—this party will be my ruin.

ARAMIS

No, since I am here—and don't I have behind me a rich and powerful party interested in keeping you when you are? Fear nothing, and don't forget your letter to la Vallière.

FOUQUET

(calling)

Toby.

TOBY

(appearing)

Sir?

FOUQUET

Come, I have to confide a message of importance to you.

USHER

(announcing)

Her Royal Highness, Madame.

(Madame Henriette enters accompanied by de Vardes)

DE VARDES

Madame, following your instructions the Count de le Fère is waiting for the moment to present himself before His Majesty.

MADAME

You will go find Mr. de la Fère after my plan has succeeded.

KING

(low to Saint-Aignan)

Oh, Saint-Aignan, see how charming Miss de la Vallière is.

SAINT-AIGNAN

Sire, pay attention to Madame!

MADAME

(to her ladies of honor)

Ladies—don't forget that we are agreed on the subject of the incident at the royal oak—His Majesty is persuaded no one knows of His action?

LOUISE

Ah, Madame—I swear to you it's true!

MADAME

So be it—but I pretend, I pretend, do you clearly understand? Let His Majesty return to this thought—and for that, you must do what I demand. You must support boldly what you all three knew perfectly well: the presence of the King and that of Mr. Saint-Aignan behind the oak—

LOUISE

But Madame—that's to toy with the King—to lie—

MADAME

If Miss de Bragellone le Blanca de la Vallière—doesn't wish to lie, she'll approve of my sending her to her vales of Turaine or Blaisons—down there, quite at her ease, she can give in to sentiments and pastorals—

(aside)

And thanks to the measures I've taken that won't be long delayed.

(to the King who returns from the back)

With the permission of Your Majesty we have a surprise with which we wish to entertain the King.

KING

A surprise.

MADAME

Yes, Sire, a tale. Oh, it will be short and interesting.

KING

Let's see the tale.

MADAME

It's a question of a little naiad I had the occasion to listen to quite recently in the forest, not far from an oak—that's called, I think, the King's oak—right, Mr. Saint-Aignan?

SAINT-AIGNAN

But Madame—

DE VARDES

(low)

Good, Madame, good—

MADAME

"Imagine, princess," the Naiad told me, "The shores of my stream have just been witness to one of the most amusing spectacles, two shepherds—curious to the point of indiscretion, got themselves hoaxed in a way to delight three nymphs or three shepherdesses..

KING

(aside, angrily)

Hoaxed!

SAINT-AIGNAN

(aside)

Ah, my God!

MADAME

The two shepherds, pursuing my pretty naiad, laughing all the while, followed the tracks of the ladies—but the shepherdesses had seen Tyrcis and Amyntas slip into the woods, and the moon helping—they recognized them through the trees.

KING

(aside)

They recognized me!

SAINT-AIGNAN

Ah! My God! Ah! My God!

DE VARDES

(low)

Courage, Madame.

MADAME

The shepherdesses—seeing the indiscretion of the shepherds, went to sit at the foot of the royal oak, and then, perceiving the shepherds were cocking their ears, so as not to lose a word of what was being said, the shepherdesses addressed them innocently, in the most artless way in the world—an incendiary declaration which due to the vanity natural to all men, seemed to the two auditors like rays of honey.

KING

(rising),

Ah! There, on my word, is a charming joke, and told by you Madame in a way no less charming—But really, really indeed, do you understand the language of the naiads?

MADAME

Sire, as I feared, indeed, to have misunderstood, I made Miss de Montalair, Miss de Tonnay Chacente and Miss de la Vallière—come pray to my naiads to retell her tale. She obeyed and I affirm to you that there's no doubt remaining—right ladies, didn't the naiad speak absolutely as I am telling and that in no way have I fallen short of the truth? Miss de Tonnay—is it true?

ATHÉNAÏS

The precise truth.

MADAME

Is it true, Miss de Montalair?

AURE

Oh, absolutely, Madame.

MADAME

And you, la Vallière?

LOUISE

Yes.

KING

(aside)

She knew! She doesn't love me! This was an unworthy comedy!

DE VARDES

(low to Madame)

You triumph!

MADAME

Mr. de Vardes go find the Comte de la Fère.

(de Vardes leaves)

The story of my naiad has pleased the King?

KING

Surely, Madame—and even better, it was all the more humorous (low) vicious (aloud) and no one—no one can contest her proof.

MADAME

Now, Sire, is it permitted for me to solicit a few minutes of audience for the Count de la Fère?

KING

An audience—at this moment?

MADAME

It's a matter that concerns the happiness to one of your best gentlemen—and in which I myself take a great interest . Here's Mr. de la Fère—

ATHOS

(presented by Mr. Vardes)

Sire.

KING

(impatiently)

Well, Mr. de la Fère—what's wrong?

ATHOS

The King recalls doubtless that at the Louvre, I had the honor of addressing to His Majesty a request concerning the marriage of my son with Miss de la Vallière.

KING

(hesitating)

Ah—indeed, sir, I think I recall.

ATHOS

Your Majesty, said that he was delaying this marriage for the good of Mr. de Bragellone. Today my son is so wretched that I was unable to defer any longer requesting a solution. I am coming from London with my son. Madame who had knowledge of our arrival deigned to order me near her and promised me her assistance. It's to her kindness that I owe the power to speak at this moment to Your Majesty—excuse my importunity, Sire—and deign to pronounce a judgment favorable to my son—

KING

I have no judgment to pronounce. Miss de la Vallière is not part of my house—if Madame, if Miss de la Vallière desire it—

ATHOS

Your Majesty is not opposed? The King consents?

KING

I have no opposition to make nor consent to give.

ATHOS

Then Your Majesty will look on this marriage without displeasure?

KING

Yes, sir—goodbye, Count—

ATHOS

(bowing)

Sire!

(The King leaves—looking at Miss de la Vallière, who remains—annihilated.)

MADAME

(to Athos—after the King has moved away)

Well, Mr. de la Fère—are you satisfied?

ATHOS

Madame, I'm off to instruct my son of the happiness he owes to you and I'll return with him to place at the feet of Your Royal Highness our respect and our gratitude.

MADAME

Go—Mr. de la Fère—

DE VARDES

(low to Madame)

Well played, Madame!

LOUISE

(supported by Aure and Athénaïs)

Oh, I think I'm going to die!

CURTAIN

ACT III
SCENE 5

The apartment of the maids of honor in the palace at Fontainebleau.

QUEEN

Let's stop, Mr. Colbert.

COLBERT

Are you ill, Madame?

QUEEN

Yes, indeed.

COLBERT

Would you like me to inform The Doctor—? He's in Madame's apartment.

QUEEN

No need, Mr. Colbert—I feel better—anyway, it's not a Doctor who must come cure me. They told me of a woman from

Bruges who effects miraculous cures and I ordered this woman to Fontainebleau. I'm expecting her—but let's get back to our affairs—Now, Mr. Colbert, I won't hide from you that the King appears to me to have the best intentions with regard to Mr. Fouquet and I think you will do well—faced with such an example, to depart a little from your feelings of hate.

COLBERT

Madame, it's note hate which animates me, but a conviction.

QUEEN

A conviction?

COLBERT

Yes, Madame; I am convinced that Mr. Fouquet not content to attract money to himself as Cardinal Mazarin did—and to thus deprive the King of a share of his power—still wants to win all the friends of the easy life and life of pleasure—I am convinced that Mr. Fouquet infringes on the royal prerogative and is trying to relegate His Majesty among the weak and obscure—and it's because I am convinced of that that I am fighting this colossus of pride! In acting thus, I have in view, not the satisfaction of a personal hate, but only service to the good of the state and moreover the glory and honor of the royal authority.

QUEEN

Solely?— I want to believe you, Mr. Colbert.

COLBERT

But you yourself, Madame?

QUEEN

Oh, sir, I too, I admit that I have been the enemy of the superintendent, but it was when my son found himself, in guardianship without resources, without authority; as a mother, I suffered as queen, I was humiliated—the future seemed to me—forbidding and worrisome. Today, my son no longer takes advice, that is to say, the orders of Mazarin! He is master, he is King! I no longer tremble; I no longer suffer; my pride, my legitimate pride has recovered and I can see shine beneath the royal splendor of Louis XIV, the magnificence of Superintendent Fouquet.

COLBERT

(aside)

No matter! Let a proof come, a weapon against Mr. Fouquet and I won't allow either the weapon or the evidence to escape.

A SERVANT (woman) of the Queen

Madame, the Lady from Bruges is here, she's awaiting the good pleasure of Your Majesty.

QUEEN

Have her come.

(she moves toward the rear, meanwhile Toby enters by a side door)

TOBY

(to Colbert)

Milord, I was looking for you. This letter they entrusted me with. Take it! Take it!

COLBERT

(looking at the letter)

From the Superintendent to Miss de la Vallière! Ah, thanks Toby—I won't forget it—The evidence that I was waiting for—here it is! Mr. Fouquet you are ruined!

(A masked lady enters.)

QUEEN

Approach. Who are you?

LADY

A wise woman from Bruges and I bring the remedy that must cure Your Majesty.

QUEEN

You don't know that one doesn't speak to royal personages with a mask on your face.

LADY

Deign to excuse me, Madame.

QUEEN

I cannot excuse you. I cannot pardon you unless you remove this mask.

LADY

It's a vow I took, Madame—to come to the aid of persons afflicted or suffering without their ever seeing my face.

QUEEN

Ah! Well, speak—

LADY

When we are alone—

(at a sign from the Queen the company moves away)

QUEEN

Now, speak, Madame—and may you be able, as you just said, to bring ease to my body.

LADY

Question, first of all. What disaster happened to Your Majesty 23 years ago?

QUEEN

Why—great misfortune! Didn't I lose the King?

LADY

I wasn't speaking of that sort of misfortune. I meant to ask you—if, after the birth of the King?

QUEEN

I don't comprehend you.

LADY

I am going to make myself understood. Your Majesty recalls that the King was born on the 5th of September 1638 at 11:15.

QUEEN

Everyone knows that as well as you and me—

LADY

Madame, I'm getting to what few persons know since the secret was assured by the death of the principal participants.

QUEEN

(attentive)

Continue—

LADY

It was 8 o'clock; the King sighed with a full heart; there was only joy around him. Suddenly, Your Majesty let out a piercing shriek and the midwife Peronne reappeared at her bedside. The doctors were dining in a far off room—the palace, deserted, had neither orders nor guards; the midwife after having examined Your Majesty's condition, exclaimed and taking you in her arms—in tears—sent La Porte to inform the King that Her Majesty, the Queen, wished to see him in her chamber; the King arrived at the minute Dame Peronne handed him a second prince, handsome and strong as the first—saying, "Sire, God didn't want the Kingdom of France to be ruled by women." The King had at first made a movement of joy, then he reflected that two sons, in equal rights, equal in pretensions—would be civil war, anarchy—and then—

QUEEN

(agitated)

And then?

LADY

Then, needing only the first born, they hid the second from France—they hid him from the whole world.

QUEEN

You know much—since you touch on secrets of State. As for the friends who share this secret with you—they are cowards and false friends. Now—down with the mask or I'll have you arrested by my captain of the guards—oh—that secret doesn't frighten me! You will reveal it to me—it will freeze in your breast! Neither this secret nor your life belong to you—from this moment.

LADY

Madame, learn to know the discretion of your abandoned friends.

QUEEN

Madame de Chevreuse.

LADY

The sole confidant of Your Majesty's secret.

QUEEN

Ah, pardon—Duchess. Alas, it's to kill one's friends to play with their mortal shame.

DUCHESS

You are weeping! How young you are still!

QUEEN

So you've come—you! you!

DUCHESS

Yes, Madame, I come despite the order that condemned me to exile, I come because I am growing old, because I feel ill, and because I wanted, before dying to deliver to Your Majesty a certain dangerous paper—dangerous for her—

QUEEN

A dangerous paper?

DUCHESS

Yes, it's a letter dated Tuesday, August 2nd, 1644 whereby you request me to go to Noisy-le-Sec—to see this dear, unfortunate child—it was in your handwriting, Madame, "This dear, unfortunate child."

QUEEN

Yes, unfortunate—really unfortunate. What a life to terminate in such a cruel end.

DUCHESS

Then you think he's dead?

QUEEN

Alas, yes! Dead of consumption—dead at Noisy-le-Sec in the arms of the governor, poor honest servant—who didn't live long afterwards.

DUCHESS

Well, no, Madame, no, your child didn't die at Noisy-le Sec.

QUEEN

What are you saying?

DUCHESS

I'm saying that you were deceived. He's been carried off, hidden, moved away—but all that I've learned gives me the conviction that he exists.

QUEEN

He exists?

DUCHESS

Yes, Madame, I believe so—I am sure of it.

QUEEN

Then—where is he?

DUCHESS

I don't know—I've never learned.

QUEEN

Well, as for me, I will search, I will find him—yes, he must exist, poor child! Ah, you didn't think I would willingly let him vegetate far from the throne? You didn't think I could be a bad mother? You know—how many tears I shed, you were able to count the ardent kisses I gave to the poor creature in exchange for the life of misery and opprobrium to which the reason of State condemned him. But if he's still in the world, Lord, my God be blessed! What I will do for him, I don't know, but I will love him—I—Oh—he exists—he exists—poor child! Now, Duchess, your arm—escort me to my apartment and tell me what I can do for you.

DUCHESS

A single thing, Madame, speak to the King in my favor—beg him to end my exile.

QUEEN

What you wish for me to do, I will attempt. My God—how upset I am—come—I can refuse nothing to she who put in my heart this hope that my poor child still lives—come—come!

(They leave.)

(The King appears at another door on the left.)

KING

(to Miss de Montalais)

Miss de la Vallière?

AURE

She's here, Sire.

(She leaves, Louise appears immediately.)

KING

You wrote me, Miss? What do you want?

LOUISE

Sire, pardon me!

KING

Eh, Miss—why do you want me to pardon you?

LOUISE

Sire, I've committed a great fault, more than a great fault—a great crime.

KING

You?

LOUISE

I've offended Your Majesty.

KING

Not the least in the world.

LOUISE

Sire, I beg you, don't keep vis-à-vis me this terrible gravity which betrays the very legitimate wrath of the King, I feel that I have offended you, but I need to explain to you, Sire, I didn't offend you of my own will.

KING

And, first of all, Miss—in what could you have offended me? I don't see it. It's a joke by a young girl? A very innocent joke! You scoffed at a credulous man. That's very natural. All other women in your place would have done as you did.

LOUISE

Your Majesty annihilates me with those words.

KING

In what way?

LOUISE

Because if the joke came from me, it would not have been innocent.

KING

Finally, is this all you had to say to me in asking for this audience?

LOUISE

Your Majesty understood everything?

KING

Everything—what?

LOUISE

Everything said by me under the Royal Oak?

KING

I didn't miss a single word, Miss.

LOUISE

And Your Majesty doesn't suspect that a poor girl like me may sometimes be forced to submit to the will of others?

KING

Pardon, but I will never understand how a will seemingly so freely expressed under the Royal Oak, allows itself to be influenced to this degree by the will of others.

LOUISE

Oh, but threats, Sire.

KING

Threats! Who threatened you—who dared threaten you?

LOUISE

Those who have the right to do so, Sire.

KING

I don't consider anyone has the right to make threats in my court.

LOUISE

Pardon me, Sire, there are near Your Majesty persons sufficiently highly placed to have, or think they have the right to ruin a young girl without a future, without a fortune—who has only her reputation.

KING

And how would she be ruined?

LOUISE

By inflicting on her a shameful expulsion.

KING

(bitterly)

Ah, Miss, I really like people who exculpate themselves without incriminating others.

LOUISE

Sire!

KING

Yes, and it's my fault, I admit it, to see an easy justification, as yours could be—coming to complicate things for me with a veil of reproaches and accusations.

LOUISE

To whom don't you give credit, then?

(the King remains silent)

Oh! Say it!

KING

I regret admitting it to you.

LOUISE

Then you don't believe me?

(silence)

So you imagine that I—I—I hatched this ridiculous, this infamous conspiracy to make me behave so impudently before Your Majesty?

KING

Eh! My God! It's not ridiculous, it's not infamous—it's not even a conspiracy! It's a joke—more or less pleasant, that's all.

LOUISE

(desperate)

Oh! The King doesn't believe me! The King doesn't want to believe me.

KING

No indeed, I don't want to, I cannot believe you.

LOUISE

My God! My God!

KING

What could be more natural, indeed? You said to yourself, "The King follows me, listens to me, lies in wait for me; the King perhaps wants to amuse himself at my expense—let's amuse ourselves at his—and as the King is a man of heart let's use the way of the heart. Let's make up this fable—that I love him, and that I singled him out. The King is so naive and so proud at the same time, that he'll believe me and then we'll go tell about this naivety of the King—and we'll laugh!"

LOUISE

Ah, to think like that is terrible.

KING

"And that's not all: if this proud prince comes to take this joke seriously, if he's so imprudent as to publicly show some thing—like joy—well before the whole court the King will be humiliated for this one day will be a charming tale to tell my lover—a share of the dowry I will bring my husband"—this adventure of a King mocked by a malicious young girl.

LOUISE

Sire, I beg you—can't you see you are killing me?

KING

Oh—joking.

LOUISE

(falling on her knees and joining her hands)

Sire, I prefer shame to treason.

KING

What are you doing?

LOUISE

Sire, when I've sacrificed my honor and my reason to you, perhaps you'll believe in my honesty. The tale was made up at Madame's and by Madame—and it is a lie—and what I told you under the great oak—

KING

Well—?

LOUISE

That alone—is the truth.

KING

Miss.

LOUISE

Sire, so I must die of shame on this spot, I will repeat to you until my voice fails me, I told you that I love you—well, I love you!

KING

You?

LOUISE

I love you, Sire, since the day I saw you—when at Blois—your royal glance fell on me, I love you, Sire! It's a crime of lese majesty, I know, for a poor girl like me to love her King and to tell him so. Punish me for this audacity, scorn me for this imprudence, but don't ever say, don't ever believe that I mocked you, that I betrayed you. I come from blood loyal to royalty, Sire—and I love—I love my King! Ah! I am dying.

(she faints)

KING

Help! Someone! She's going to die.

(to Aure and Saint-Aignan who come up running)

AURE

Louise! Louise!

LOUISE

Ah! Sire! Your Majesty has pardoned me then?

(getting up)

Now, Sire, now—allow me to retire to a convent! I shall bless my King all my life—and I will die loving God, who gave me a day of happiness.

KING

No, no, you will live here, blessing God on the contrary, but loving Louis who will give you a happy life; Louis who loves you with all the strength God has put in him. Louis who will give his life smiling if you ask it of him.

(he takes her in his arms)

LOUISE

Oh, Sire, don't make me repent of having been so honest—for that would prove to me that Your Majesty scorns me still.

KING

Miss—I honor and love nothing in this world more than you—and no other woman at my court—I swear to God—will be as esteemed as you will be henceforth—I ask your pardon for my distraction—it comes from an excess of love.

(bowing to her and taking her hand)

Miss will you do me the honor of consenting to the kiss that I place on your hand?

(he kisses her hand)

From this moment, you are under my protection, don't speak to anyone of the wrong I did you; forgive what others did to you. In the future you will be so far above them, far from inspiring fear in you, they will only make you pity them the more.

(to Saint-Aignan)

Count, I hope Miss will willingly grant you a bit of her friendship—in return for that I've vowed to her forever—

SAINT-AIGNAN

(bending his knee to La Vallière)

What joy for me, if Miss will do me such an honor—

KING

(seeing Aure who has come forward)

Miss de Montalais.

LOUISE

Sire—a friend who's been faithful to me—always.

KING

I won't forget her.

AURE

Sire!

KING

(to Louise)

Miss—goodbye or rather au revoir! Do me the kindness of not forgetting me in your heart—

LOUISE

Sire, you are with God in my heart.

AURE

(aside)

Well, this is an ending Madame Henriette didn't foresee.

(Louise goes to the rear accompanying the King—she casts a glance at the side door and lets out an exclamation.)

KING

What's the matter—?

(seeing Athos)

Mr. de la Fère!

ATHOS

Sire, excuse me; I am authorized to enter the apartment of the ladies of honor—while my son is still with Madame, I was coming to announce to Miss de la Vallière the visit of her fiancé—

KING

Her fiancé?

LOUISE

My God!

ATHOS

What's wrong with you, Miss? This news seems to produce a strange reaction in you. Your intentions are no longer the same as at Blois? Must I recall your plans, your oaths? As for my son —he hasn't forgotten them—What's going on?—Am I wrong to bring these flattering promises to Raoul?

LOUISE

Count.

(she looks to the King beseechingly)

KING

Promises, sir—say hopes—

ATHOS

(looking at the King)

Still it seems to me that in the presence of Madame, Your Majesty said —.

KING

(excitedly)

Me—I didn't say a thing—

ATHOS

Madame just now affirmed to me—

KING

(excitedly)

Madame—Madame—

(aside)

Now I understand—Louise was right, Madame planned it all—it's a conspiracy—I will thwart it—

ATHOS

(looking alternatively to the King and Louise)

Finally, Sire, pardon me for addressing Your Majesty—has some obstacle suddenly arisen?

KING

Perhaps—

ATHOS

And this obstacle is—?

KING

It's—it's my will—

ATHOS

The will of the King? But this morning when I solicited Your Majesty to reveal your will to me, the King informed me he had none.

KING

This morning—yes—Now—

ATHOS

Now what does the King want? Does he deign to consent?— the King hesitates—

KING

I don't hesitate—I refuse.

LOUISE

(joyfully)

Ah!

ATHOS

Sire—

KING

You still have something to say to me, Count?

ATHOS

Yes, Sire.

KING

(to Louise)

Go, Miss—

(Louise leaves, giving the King a sign of gratitude.)

KING

Well, sir, I'm waiting.

ATHOS

Sire, may I be permitted to humbly ask Your Majesty this reason for his refusal?

KING

The reason—a question.

ATHOS

A demand, Sire?

KING

You've forgotten the custom the court, Mr. de la Fère—in the court, no one questions the King.

ATHOS

That's true, Sire—but if no one questions him—they conjecture.

KING

They conjecture—what's that mean?

ATHOS

Sire, instead of having a response from Your Majesty on the sudden change that's just taken place—I am forced to reply to myself.

KING

Sir, I've given you all the free time I have.

ATHOS

Sire, I haven't had the time to tell the King what I have to tell him—which bursts from my heart.

KING

You were making conjectures—you are going to pass to offenses?

ATHOS

Oh, Sire, offend the King—me? Never—never would I believe that my King, when he gave me his word, would conceal an ulterior motive with his word.

KING

What's that mean—an ulterior motive?

ATHOS

That by refusing my son the hand of Miss de la Vallière, Your Majesty had some other end than his happiness and his future.

KING

You see clearly, sir, you are offending me.

ATHOS

That, finally in asking a delay, Your Majesty only wanted to separate the fiancé from Miss de la Vallière—

KING

Sir—

ATHOS

That's what I've heard said by everyone, Sire—everywhere they talk of the love of Your Majesty for Miss de la Vallière—and what happened just now is the proof of it.

KING

Ill luck to those who meddle in my affairs—I've taken a decision—I will destroy all obstacles.

ATHOS

What obstacles?

KING

I love Miss de la Vallière—

ATHOS

Well, sacrifice your love, Sire. The sacrifice is worthy of a King—it is deserved by my services and my devotion. The King by renouncing his love will prove at the same time his generosity, his gratitude and his political sagacity.

KING

Eh! Well, Miss de la Vallière doesn't love Mr. de Bragellone.

ATHOS

The King knows that?

KING

I know it.

ATHOS

For a short while then—without that, if the King knew that at my first request, His Majesty would have taken the trouble to tell me?

KING

For a short while.

ATHOS

I don't understand then why the King knowing of it sent Mr. de Bragellone to London: that exile, rightfully surprises those who love the honor of the King.

KING

Who speaks of the honor of the King, sir?

ATHOS

The honor of the King, sir, is made from the honor of all his nobility—when the King offends one of his gentlemen, that is to say when he takes a scrap of his honor—it's he himself, that is the King whose share of honor is stolen.

KING

Mr. de la Fère!

ATHOS

Sire, I am old and I cling to all was truly great and truly strong in the realm. I poured out my blood for your father and for you without asking anything of you or your father—I've never done wrong to anyone and I've obliged Kings! You shall listen to me! Today, before the entire court, you gave to my son consent. So be it——but on behalf of the King, that was enough. Now you've withdrawn this consent to serve your love—your weakness—that's bad. I know these words irritate Your Majesty, but the facts kill us—I know that you are seeking some punishment to subdue my frankness—but I know the punishment I shall ask God to inflict on you when I tell him your sin and the wrong to my son. Goodbye, Sire.

(Athos leaves.)

KING

(calling in anger)

Mr. D'Artagnan.

D'ARTAGNAN

(entering)

Here I am.

KING

I just left Mr. de la Fère—who is an insolent fellow.

D'ARTAGNAN

An insolent fellow?

KING

If you are loath to arrest him yourself, send some other officer.

D'ARTAGNAN

There is no need for another office, since I am on duty.

KING

The Count is your friend.

D'ARTAGNAN

If he were my father, I would still be on duty.

KING

What are you waiting for?

D'ARTAGNAN

The signed order.

KING

(writing hurriedly)

Here it is.

D'ARTAGNAN

Sire—have you really considered?

KING

Sir—are you going to brave me, too?

D'ARTAGNAN

I am counting on that, indeed, Sire, for once you've taken that fine action, you wouldn't even dare to look me in the face again.

(The King tosses his pen away violently.)

KING

Get out!

D'ARTAGNAN

Oh, not at all, Sire—if it pleases Your Majesty.

KING

What do you mean, not at all?

D'ARTAGNAN

Sire, I came to speak softly to the King—the King is distracted—that's unfortunate, but I won't say less to the King than what I have to tell him.

KING

Your resignation, sir, your resignation?

D'ARTAGNAN

Sire you know that my discharge isn't dear to my heart, since that day at Blois, when Your Majesty refused to King Charles the II the million which the Count, my friend gave him—I offered my resignation to the King.

KING

Well, then, make it quick.

D'ARTAGNAN

No, Sire, for it's not my resignation which is in question here; Your Majesty took up the pen to place me in the Bastille—what's changed his opinion?

KING

D'Artagnan, bull headed Gascon! Who is the King here—you or me? Look!

D'ARTAGNAN

It's you, Sire, unfortunately!

KING

What do you mean, unfortunately?

D'ARTAGNAN

Yes, Sire, for if it was me—

KING

If it was you, you would approve the rebellion of Mr. D'Artagnan, right?

D'ARTAGNAN

Yes, surely—

KING

Honestly?

D'ARTAGNAN

And I would say to my Captain-General of the Musketeers—I would tell him—looking at him with kindly eyes—I would say to him "Mr. D'Artagnan, I'd forgotten that I am the King, I descended from my throne to outrage a gentleman—"

KING

Sir, do you think to excuse your friend by surpassing him in insolence?

D'ARTAGNAN

Oh, Sire—I will really go much farther than he—I will tell

you what he didn't tell you. Sire, you've sacrificed the Count de la Fère; he spoke to you in the name of honor, of religion and virtue—you repulsed him, kicked him out, imprisoned him!

As for me, I will be more hard then he—and I will say to you—choose—do you want people to serve you or do you want them to bend to you? Do you want them to love you or do you want them to fear you? If you prefer baseness, intrigue, cowardice, oh—say so, Sire; we will leave, the rest of us—those who remain—I will tell you more—the only models of valor in the past, we who served and perhaps surpassed in courage, in merit—men already great to posterity—choose, Sire, and hurry—those of your great lords remaining—keep them—you will still have plenty of courtiers—hurry and send me to the Bastille with my friend—that's what I have to tell you—pardon me, Sire, you were at fault to push me to do it.

(He draws his sword and respectfully approaches Louis XIV, places it on the table. The King with a ferocious gesture pushes it away—and the sword falls on the floor and rolls to D'Artagnan's feet. The latter, after a moment of stupefaction takes it up with emotion.)

D'ARTAGNAN

A king can disgrace a soldier, he can exile him, he can condemn him to death, but were he a hundred times King, he has no right to insult him by dishonoring his sword. Sire, a King of France has never repulsed with scorn the sword of a man like me. This soiled sword, think of it, Sire, it has no other scabbard now than my heart. May my blood fall back on your head!

(With a rapid gesture, leaning the hilt of the sword on the floor, he turns the point on his breast. The King rushes with an even more rapid movement than D'Artagnan's, throws his right hand on D'Artagnan's neck and his left seizes the middle of the blade of the sword and silently replaces it in the scabbard—then softened, returns to the table and tears up the order.)

KING

Mr. D'Artagnan, your friend is free!

(D'Artagnan seizes the royal hand, kisses it and leaves without a word.)

CURTAIN

ACT IV
SCENE 6

The Bastille—same as in the third scene.

MONTLEZUN

(at dinner with Aramis)

Come, Chevalier, to you health!

ARAMIS

(to a servant who enters)

Well, what is it?

VALET

A message that a courier just brought from Fontainebleau.

MONTLEZUN

(after having torn open the envelope)

A release order. Did you ever? Nice news to disturb us with.

ARAMIS

Admit at least, that it's good for the one concerned.

MONTLEZUN

At 9:30 in the evening!

ARAMIS

Come—some charity!

MONTLEZUN

From charity, I wish him well—but it's for this comedian who's bored—not for me who amuse myself.

ARAMIS

Is it a loss that you are going to have—?

MONTLEZUN

Ah, indeed yes, a three pound note, but still since the detainee interests you—

ARAMIS

As for me, I don't know him, but like the poet Terence, "I am a man and nothing human is foreign to me."

(opening the paper and reading)

MONTLEZUN

Tomorrow, at daybreak, he shall leave.

ARAMIS

Why not tonight? At the top of the letter is the word "expedite."

MONTLEZUN

Yes, but tonight we are dining and we are in a hurry, too.

ARAMIS

Dear Montlezun, charity is a duty more imperious than hunger and thirst—how long has this wretch been a prisoner?

MONTLEZUN

For 10 years.

ARAMIS

Ten years, that's long! Shorten his suffering by a dozen hours—a nice moment awaits him—give it to him quickly.

MONTLEZUN

You wish it?

ARAMIS

I beg you—

MONTLEZUN

Like that—ruining dinner?

ARAMIS

I beseech you—

MONTLEZUN

Then let it be as you wish—François! François! Well—the comedian doesn't come!

(he rises to go to the door and call François, Aramis replaces the order with a similar one, François appears)

François let them bring the Major with his turnkeys from la Berthandière.

ARAMIS

If you make them open his prison right away—we'll announce this news ourselves to the poor devil.

MONTLEZUN

François, the Major will open the prison of Mr. Seldon, #3 la Berthandière.

ARAMIS

Seldon, you said Seldon, I think?

MONTLEZUN

I said Seldon—that's the name of the one to be released.

ARAMIS

You mean Marchiali?

MONTLEZUN

Marchiali—ah, indeed, yes! So—Seldon.

ARAMIS

I think you are making an error, my dear Montlezun.

MONTLEZUN

I read the order.

ARAMIS

I, too.

MONTLEZUN

And I saw Seldon in big letters like this.

(points with his finger)

ARAMIS

(also pointing)

And, I, Marchiali in large characters like this.

MONTLEZUN

Let's clarify this—it's quite easy. There's the paper—let's read.

ARAMIS

(unfolding the paper)

I read "Marchiali".

MONTLEZUN

(reading)

"Marchiali" yes, indeed it is Marchiali.

ARAMIS

You see?

MONTLEZUN

(astonished)

Why the one they fear so much—the one they commended to me so carefully.

ARAMIS

(insisting)

It's Marchiali then?

MONTLEZUN

I have to admit that's phenomenal. I saw the order and the name Seldon. I see it and I even recall it under the name—there was a blot of ink.

ARAMIS

Still, although you have seen it, dear Mr. de Montlezun, the order is signed to deliver Marchiali with or without a blot and there's the order. You are going to free this prisoner. If your heart tells you to free Seldon at the same time, do it; I declare to you I am not opposed in any manner since, as you recall, Seldon was recommended to me.

MONTLEZUN

I will free the prisoner Marchiali after I've recalled the courier who brought the order and interrogated him so I will be assured....

ARAMIS

(interrupting him)

The order was sealed and the courier ignorant of the contents; of what can you assure yourself—? Speak.

MONTLEZUN

If necessary, I will send to the ministry and Mr. de Lionne to redo the order or confirm it.

ARAMIS

What's the good of that?

MONTLEZUN

To assure myself I am obeying—not indeed some false order, but indeed the order of my superiors.

ARAMIS

And your superiors are?

MONTLEZUN

Mr. de Lionne, first of all—

ARAMIS

And above Mr. de Lionne?

MONTLEZUN

The King.

ARAMIS

Isn't there yet another whom you ought to obey?

MONTLEZUN

(terrified)

Sir! Sir!

ARAMIS

Don't you belong to a mysterious organization? Say yes—say no—but say one or the other—we have no time to lose.

MONTLEZUN

Pardon, sir—but—

ARAMIS

Drink a glass of this excellent Muscatel, Montlezun—you seem terrified my friend.

FRANÇOIS

Governor, here's a number 3 from Berthandière, they are bringing—

ARAMIS

(coldly)

Tell them it's a mistake and it's not him—we have not resolved the question I am putting to you—when you've answered yes or no, well—you will decide—

MONTLEZUN

Take the prisoner back to his room and wait for new orders.

ARAMIS

Very well!

(François leaves)

MONTLEZUN

My God!

ARAMIS

(insisting)

Ah—then you belong to this organization?

MONTLEZUN

Me?

ARAMIS

You admitted that a moment ago by sending the prisoner Seldon to his room—you obeyed the order that the organization gave you by way of my mouth. Well, you know one thing, dear Mr. de Montlezun—it's that you can't be linked to an organization to enjoy the advantages it produces for its members as for example paying 150,000 for him without being compelled oneself to some little services.

MONTLEZUN

In those circumstances, still—sir—

ARAMIS

Then there is an engagement taken by all governors and captains of affiliated fortresses to obey all orders—verbal or written—

MONTLEZUN

Yes—but you don't have that order.

ARAMIS

Here it is! Ah, yes, it's true the seal is missing—

(he takes some wax—plans a seal on it with his ring, then shows it to the stupefied Montlezun)

Come, come, don't make me believe Mr. de Montlezun that the presence of the Chief is terrible like that of God and that one dies having seen him.

(with severity)

It's true one might die and certainly would die for not having obeyed him—get up then and obey!

MONTLEZUN

Oh—I'll never recover from such a blow! I who joked with you—I who dared treat you on a footing of equality—

ARAMIS

Recall François.

MONTLEZUN

And—

ARAMIS

And obey the order of the King countersigned by de Lionne.

MONTLEZUN

(going to the door, to François who enters)

Bring here #2 Berthandière.

ARAMIS

Marvelous, my dear Montlezun. Well, you see it wasn't as difficult as all that.

MONTLEZUN

Yes, but the consequences?

ARAMIS

You are naive, Mr. de Montlezun—don't bother reflecting when others take the trouble to think for you. Anyway who knows what this order will accomplish?

MONTLEZUN

What do you mean?

ARAMIS

Yes—everything's going to depend on my conversation with this young man. After 10 minutes of conversation, perhaps you will say—"This order is false. Take this prisoner back to his room."

MONTLEZUN

(joyous)

Oh!

ARAMIS

But then again, after these 10 minutes of conversation, perhaps I shall tell you, "This order is good. Release the prisoner."

MONTLEZUN

And me, during this time?

ARAMIS

You will stay by this door—you will guard us and you will make sure no one hears us.

MONTLEZUN

Here's the prisoner.

(Marchiali enters.)

ARAMIS

Withdraw and leave us alone.

(Montlezun leaves)

ARAMIS

(after giving Marchiali a sign to sit down)

Sir, you received, yesterday, a letter in your bread?

MARCHIALI

Yes, sir—

ARAMIS

That letter announced to you there was going to be a great change in your destiny?

MARCHIALI

Yes, sir—

ARAMIS

That a man would come to the Bastille who would have an important revelation to make you.

MARCHIALI

Yes, sir.

ARAMIS

I am that man.

MARCHIALI

I am listening.

ARAMIS

The last time that I had the honor of seeing you, a third was present, who, of necessity, stopped in my lips and on yours complete confidence ready to leave, all secrets ready to escape.

MARCHIALI

I don't have any secrets to keep nor confidences to make, there was no constraint on my part.

ARAMIS

The first time I had the honor to see you, I asked you what was the crime you committed that placed you in the Bastille and you evaded replying—permit me to renew the same question.

MARCHIALI

And why do you think that I should have more confidence in you today than a week ago?

ARAMIS

Because we are alone and you received a letter that informed you of my visit.

MARCHIALI

That letter was not signed; as for you—I don't know you—

ARAMIS

So you refuse to confess to me the crime you committed?

MARCHIALI

If you want me to tell you what crime I committed, explain to me what a crime is as I feel nothing in me to reproach myself with—I tell myself that I am not a criminal.

ARAMIS

Sometimes one is a criminal in the eyes of the great of the Earth, not only for having committed a crime but because you know that a crime has been committed.

MARCHIALI

You are right, sir—and it would be in this that I become criminal in the eyes of the greats of the Earth.

ARAMIS

Ah—you know something?

MARCHIALI

No—I know nothing—but I think sometimes and I tell myself—

ARAMIS

What do you say to yourself?

MARCHIALI

That if I wanted to examine my thoughts or if I became insane or—

ARAMIS

Or—?

MARCHIALI

Or I could divine things—

ARAMIS

Well—then—?

MARCHIALI

Then I stop—terrified of going too far.

ARAMIS

You don't have confidence in God?

MARCHIALI

Indeed, but I fear men.

ARAMIS

Isn't God in everything?

MARCHIALI

Say at the end of all things, sir—

ARAMIS

(shivering)

So be it!

(to himself)

I am not dealing with any ordinary man—so much the better.

(aloud)

Are you ambitious?

MARCHIALI

What's ambition?

ARAMIS

It's a feeling that pushes a man to want more than he has.

MARCHIALI

I've said I was satisfied, sir, but it is possible I was mistaken. See—open my mind—I ask nothing better, sir.

ARAMIS

An ambitious man is one who lusts above his status.

MARCHIALI

I am ignorant of who I am; I cannot lust above my status.

ARAMIS

The last time that I saw you, you lied to me.

MARCHIALI

(excitedly)

Lied, me? You told me, sir, I believe, that I lied.

ARAMIS

I meant to say, sir, that you concealed from me what you know of your childhood.

MARCHIALI

A man's secrets are his own and not for the first comer—one doesn't lie by being quiet.

ARAMIS

Oh, if I dared I would take your hand and kiss it.

MARCHIALI

Kiss the hand of a prisoner—and why?

ARAMIS

You make me despair—if you knew all I've dreamed for you.

MARCHIALI

I make you despair?

ARAMIS

Yes, for sometimes I think I have the man I'm looking for in front of my eyes—and then suddenly.

MARCHIALI

And suddenly—this man disappears?

ARAMIS

Decidedly, I have nothing to say to one who distrusts me to the degree you do.

MARCHIALI

Nor I—to one who doesn't understand that a prisoner ought to be distrustful of everyone.

ARAMIS

Even of his old friends?

MARCHIALI

You are one of my old friends? You are—?

ARAMIS

Look—don't you ever recall having seen once, in the village where you spent your first childhood—

MARCHIALI

First of all—what was the name of the village?

ARAMIS

Noisy-le-Sec.

MARCHIALI

Continue, sir.

ARAMIS

Don't you recall having seen at Noisy-le-Sec 15 or 18 years ago—a cavalier who came—accompanying a lady usually dressed in a black dress with ribbons the color of fire in her hair?

MARCHIALI

Yes, once I asked the name of that Cavalier and they told me his name was the Chevalier d'Herblay.

ARAMIS

I am the Chevalier d'Herblay.

MARCHIALI

I know it; I recognized you.

ARAMIS

Well—if you know that, then I must inform you of something—it's that if the presence of the Chevalier d'Herblay here was known to the King this evening—tomorrow the Chevalier d'Herblay would see the axe of an executioner shine from the depths of a cell more somber and forlorn than yours; you can have confidence in me, I run a risk that cannot reach Your Royal Highness.

MARCHIALI

But, sir, if you know who I am, why try to make me admit it?

ARAMIS

I wanted to know if you knew yourself.

MARCHIALI

I know myself.

ARAMIS

You know then that you are the twin brother of Louis the XIV—perhaps his elder and consequently the throne of France belongs as much to you, perhaps even more to you—than Louis XIV.

MARCHIALI

I know it.

ARAMIS

In that case, you are indeed the one I seek.

(on his knees)

Your hand, Sire.

MARCHIALI

What are you doing?

ARAMIS

I am swearing devotion and fidelity to my King and I hope that he will never forget that I am the first who took this oath to him and offered his life to him in the depths of his prison.

MARCHIALI

Sir, sir, what's the use of tempting me? You said it yourself, I am in the depths of prison.

ARAMIS

Here is the order that will get you out.

MARCHIALI

Who obtained this order?

ARAMIS

I did.

MARCHIALI

My brother consented?

ARAMIS

What does it matter in what way this order got here, since it is here, since the governor is not refusing to obey it—What! You don't accept? You are not rushing to leave prison—you see a throne in view and you don't hurl yourself towards that throne?

MARCHIALI

You tell me of a throne, sir, as if I had put my foot on its first steps. But that throne is occupied—and how will you restore it to me with the rank, the right, the power, they took from me? Ah, sir, don't speak of this throne—but throw me tomorrow in some deep valley, in the depths of some deep wood, in the midst of some savage desert—give me that joy, so I can hear freely the noise of the wind in the trees, the murmur of the stream over rocks, the song of the birds in the grass or foliage—to see the azure firmament or the stormy heaven—and that's enough.— Don't promise me more—for you cannot give me more, and it would be a crime to deceive me since you say you are my friend.

ARAMIS

Milord, I admire your feeling—so proper so delicate—which dictates your words—and I am happy to have divined my King.

MARCHIALI

From mercy—don't abuse it. As for me, I tell you, I have no need of a throne to be happy.

ARAMIS

So be it, but as for me, I need you to be King for humanity to be happy.

MARCHIALI

What does humanity have to reproach my brother with?

ARAMIS

Isn't your captivity—isn't it a crime?

MARCHIALI

Oh, yes, for he could himself come to his prison to take me by the hand and say to me, "My brother, God created us to love each other and not to fight each other, I am coming to you. A savage prejudice condemned you to perish obscurely in the depths of a cell, far from all men, deprived of all joys. Well, I want to attach you to the side of our father's sword—will you profit from my generosity to choke me; to constrain me?" Oh no—I would have replied to him: I regard you as my savior—and will respect you as my master. You will give me, indeed, more than he has given me in giving me life, since through you I have the right to love and be loved in this world.

ARAMIS

And you would have kept your word, Milord?

MARCHIALI

On my life.

ARAMIS

While now—?

MARCHIALI

Now, I feel I have to punish the guilty.

ARAMIS

Then come—don't waste time.

MARCHIALI

One word more.

ARAMIS

Speak, but let it be the last as time is running out.

MARCHIALI

When will it be noticed that the King of France is no longer Louis XIV?

ARAMIS

The King of France will still be called Louis XIV.

MARCHIALI

When will it be seen that my brother no longer reigns?

ARAMIS

Who will see it?

MARCHIALI

Why—my mother, Monsieur d'Orléans, the great dignitaries of

the realm, the royal household—the people—the whole world.

ARAMIS

Oh, my God—Is it possible that you don't know?

MARCHIALI

What?

ARAMIS

The true cause of your detention?

MARCHIALI

I told you already that I know it, sir—

ARAMIS

Have you ever seen a portrait of the King, your brother?

MARCHIALI

No never.

ARAMIS

(presenting him with a medallion)

Well—hold on—here's one.

MARCHIALI

Ah—this here is my brother?

ARAMIS

Yes and you?

MARCHIALI

Me? What do you mean?

ARAMIS

Have you sometimes looked closely in a mirror?

MARCHIALI

In the depths of a cell?

ARAMIS

(taking down a mirror and placing it before his eyes)

Then look at yourself.

MARCHIALI

(comparing the portrait with his own image)

Just God! What a resemblance!

ARAMIS

Well.

MARCHIALI

I understand everything now—oh, my brother! My brother!

ARAMIS

To you, his seat on the throne. To him, your place in this prison.

MARCHIALI

Sir, if you can restore to me the place God destined for me in the sun of fortune and glory, and if, thanks to you, I can live in the memory of men and do honor to my race by some illustrious deeds or some services rendered to my people—if from the rank prison where I languished, I am elevated to the height of honors, supported by your generous and protective hand—well, to you that I bless and thank—to you the half of my power and my glory, you will still be too little paid, for never will I succeed in sharing with you all the happiness you will have given me.

ARAMIS

Milord—your nobility of heart fills me with joy and admiration. Now—be calm—you won't be King until you've passed through the last gate of the Bastille.

MARCHIALI

I am calm: see.

ARAMIS

You will be a great King, Sire—for you are already a great heart.Montlezun!

(Montlezun enters.)

ARAMIS

My dear governor, announce yourself to this gentlemen. He is free—

MONTLEZUN

(to Marchiali)

First of all swear—it's part of the regulation that you will never reveal anything you've heard in the Bastille.

MARCHIALI

I swear it.

MONTLEZUN

You are free, then.

MARCHIALI

May God keep you in health and dignity, sir.

ARAMIS

(to Montlezun)

Wait, Montlezun—your discharge.

(leaves with the Prince)

BLACKOUT

ACT IV
SCENE 7

The Gardens of the Château at Vaux.

A party given the King by Fouquet.

Ballet of Amazons

After the divertissement the carriages of the King and Queen Mother are brought forward. Their Majesties get in the carriages, as does Madame and leave for the Hunt— preceded by a detachment of Musketeers and surrounded by the cavalcade of ladies and gentleman.

CURTAIN

ACT V
SCENE 8

The Châteaux de Vaux—the room of Morpheus.

ARAMIS

(opening a great oval window above the alcove which occupies the back of the room)

Observe, Milord.

MARCHIALI

What is this room?

ARAMIS

It's the room the King sleeps in.

MARCHIALI

And the one we are in?

ARAMIS

It's the blue room that I always occupy at the Château of Vaux—

as you see —it is above that of the King and I chose it on purpose.

MARCHIALI

You can choose them?

ARAMIS

Am I not the friend of Mr. Fouquet? Don't I dispose of everything at Vaux in his absence and act as Superintendent? In a word, didn't I organize the party? Carpenters, painters, locksmiths, mechanics, all obey my orders and you will soon see the particular way in which I've arranged the King's bed.

MARCHIALI

The King's bed?

ARAMIS

By the way—am I permitted to address a question to Your Royal Highness?

MARCHIALI

Do so.

ARAMIS

I sent to Your Highness a man of mine entrusted with delivering a notebook written carefully which will permit Your Highness to know in detail all the persons who compose and will compose his court.

MARCHIALI

I've read all those notes.

ARAMIS

Attentively?

MARCHIALI

I know them by heart.

(seeing D'Artagnan cross the room)

I recognize him from the portrait you gave me of him.

ARAMIS

Yes, Sire, Mr. D'Artagnan, your Captain-General of the Musketeers, faithful as a dog, biting sometimes. If D'Artagnan doesn't recognize you before the other has vanished—count on D'Artagnan in any extremity for then having seen nothing he will keep loyal—if he sees it too late, he's a Gascon and will never admit he was deceived.

MARCHIALI

Ah!

ARAMIS

What's wrong?

MARCHIALI

Heavens! My mother—oh—how she made me suffer. No

matter—she's my mother.

ARAMIS

Sire—no imprudence!

(he reshuts the oval window. The ladies of the court enter—preceding the Queen)

QUEEN

Look, Mr. D'Artagnan, tell me what has happened—tell me what's causing my son's fury?

D'ARTAGNAN

Madame, I suspect Mr. Colbert of having greatly antagonized the King against Mr. Fouquet.

QUEEN

Against Mr. Fouquet?

D'ARTAGNAN

Yes, Madame. They are talking about a letter from the Superintendent to Miss de la Vallière—this letter surprised by Mr. Colbert, has by him been delivered to the King. That, without doubt, is why His Majesty has ordered me to come here to await an arrest order.

QUEEN

An arrest order! Against Mr. Fouquet?

KING

(entering, to D'Artagnan)

Keep an eye on Mr. Fouquet until I've made a decision.

D'ARTAGNAN

And when will the King make his decision?

KING

This very night. And now let me be left alone.

QUEEN

Alone?

KING

I have no need of anyone.

QUEEN

Not even me?

KING

No, mother, no—I thank you.

QUEEN

A final word, my son—shall I discharge the persons gathered in the gallery—

KING

(bitterly)

No—no—let them remain—let them rejoice over the marvels of Mr. Fouquet, while awaiting the surprise I am preparing for them.

(to Saint-Aignan)

Did you inform Miss de la Vallière? Did you tell her to come here?—I want to see her—I want—ah—I am in pain.

(Everyone leaves.)

SAINT-AIGNAN

Sire—here's Miss de la Vallière.

(he leaves)

LOUISE

Sire, what's wrong with you?

KING

(with rage)

I'm suffering from humiliation.

LOUISE

From humiliation! Oh—what do you mean, Sire?

KING

I say that—here, where I am, no other should be the master. Well, see if I am not eclipsed, me, the King of France by the King of this domain. Oh, when I think this King is an unfaithful servant who waxes proud with my stolen wealth! Also, I am going to change his party to a wake,— of which the nymph of Vaux as the poets say of this impudent minister, will long preserve the memory.

LOUISE

Ah, Your Majesty.

KING

Well, Miss, are you going to take the part of Mr. Fouquet?

LOUISE

No, Sire—I will only ask of you if you are well-informed, Your Majesty has learned the value of accusations of the court—

KING

Accusations? Oh, this time I know how things stand and Mr. D'Artagnan will have terrible orders.

LOUISE

Terrible orders?

KING

Eh, yes, by God! I will tell him to arrest this titan of pride, who, faithful to his devil, threatens to scale my heaven.

LOUISE

Arrest Mr. Fouquet, who at this moment is ruining himself to do honor to his King?

KING

How you defend him!

LOUISE

Sire, it's not Mr. Fouquet I am defending, it's you yourself.

KING

Myself? You are defending me? Truly, Miss—you put a strange passion in what you say.

LOUISE

I put passion—not into what I say, Sire, but into serving Your Majesty, I'd put, if need be, my life and that with the same passion, Sire, when the King acts well—if the King wrongs me or mine, I am silent, but—if the King acts badly—I will tell him, I dare to tell him because I love him.

KING

Eh! Miss—it seems to me that Mr. Colbert, who instructed me, who revealed everything to me—it seems to me that Mr. Colbert also loves his King.

LOUISE

Yes, we both love him, each in his way. Only as for me, I love him so strongly that all the world knows it, so strongly that the

King himself doesn't doubt my love—but whatever touches his honor touches my life—so, I repeat: those who wish to dishonor the King are those who counsel him to arrest Mr. Fouquet in his home.

KING

Miss, take care I would only have to say a word.

LOUISE

Sire, don't say it; that word would be a word of wrath! Mr. Fouquet has determined enemies, I know—because the King said it, and the moment the King says it, believe. I don't require any other mouth to affirm it. But were Mr. Fouquet the last of men, were his house a den of counterfeiters—his house is sacred, his castle is inviolable, since his wife and his king are lodging here! It's a place of asylum that executioners would not violate.

KING

Well, Miss, if I am angry at Mr. Fouquet it's not because he stole my finances, it's not because with my gold, he corrupts my secretaries, generals, friends, artists—it's because he doesn't even respect my most cherished affections—it's because he dares to raise his eyes to you—actually, it's because he wrote you.

LOUISE

Wrote me?

KING

Wrote you! Do you recognize this letter?

LOUISE

This letter! How should I recognize this letter since I never received it?

KING

You never received this letter?

LOUISE

Never!

KING

Never?

LOUISE

I swear it.

KING

You swear it?

LOUISE

Before God! Do you believe me, Sire?

KING

(aside)

Her look is so pure, so shining in frankness—and love! How to suspect?

(aloud)

Louise, I believe you –yes, I believe you—this letter never reached you. It never soiled your hand or your eyes—but still—this man wrote you—I will avenge myself.

LOUISE

Oh, Sire, no vengeance. Don't cause anyone tears or sorrows—

KING

Not even—

LOUISE

Not even the author of this letter.

KING

You are the best, the sweetest of women. No one will ever have the empire over me that you do. You order me to be calm, I am calm. You want me to reign through kindness—through clemency—I will be kind and clement; you are my life—you are my soul.

LOUISE

This is really true—you love me?

KING

Yes, I love you on both knees—with all the strength God has put in my heart.

LOUISE

There I have nothing more to wish for, for your love, Sire, is all my happiness in this world.

(An usher enters.)

KING

What's wrong?

USHER

Sire, Her Highness Madame requires the services of Miss de la Vallière.

LOUISE

I am leaving my King and wish him a night full of all the feelings I myself bear away. Goodbye, Sire, goodbye.

KING

Louise—I love you—! I love you!

LaVallière offers her face—the King places a kiss on it as she flees)

(alone)

I promised her—I will pardon, Mr. Fouquet—yes, but will he pardon Colbert? Oh, I am broken—it's too much emotion.

(throwing himself on the bed)

What I am experiencing; is how annihilating it is. It seems to me I am sleeping awake—that the light is disappearing little by little—that the objects are insensibly disappearing—and that this bed itself—ah—

(his voice is snuffed out and the bed disappears under ground)

ARAMIS

(reopening the oval window and leaning out)

Porthos—are you there?

PORTHOS

(from below)

Yes.

ARAMIS

Well—

(there is a choked scream)

PORTHOS

It's done!

ARAMIS

(to Marchiali)

Now, Sire, deign to take your place in the royal bed.

MARCHIALI

I abandon myself to you—

(The oval window shuts. A bed exactly like the one that disappeared is lowered slowly from the ceiling. Marchiali is stretched out on it. Aramis is standing at the foot of the bed.)

ARAMIS

A royal tomb has just opened and shut; a new reign begins. Sire, your first minister—can he act now?

(an affirmative sign from Marchiali)

First of all, the superintendent.

(opening the door to the left)

Let someone go find Mr. Fouquet—King's order.

(returning to the desk and making the King sign a paper)

Let them have notice Mr. Baron du Vallon, candle bearer at the King's bedding—! Poor Porthos—is he going to be happy and proud!

(shouts outside)

The King! The King.

It's the people asking for Your Majesty! Go, Sire, go—everything depends on you now; you are face-to-face with your destiny—Go boldly to it!

(new shouts of Long Live the King!)

(Marchiali hesitates for a moment, then rushes through the door to the right. Aramis follows him. After a moment, the Usher, D'Artagnan and Fouquet enter.)

USHER

Enter, gentlemen and wait.

FOUQUET

(with astonishment)

The King asks to see me after having me arrested? What's it mean? Never mind—I feel I am ruined.

D'ARTAGNAN

What's happened seems to me to auger well—and yet you are sad, sir.

FOUQUET

You are mistaken, sir, I am only pensive.

D'ARTAGNAN

Your eyes follow some invisible idea.

FOUQUET

Not an idea, a phantom.

D'ARTAGNAN

And this phantom?

FOUQUET

It's my greatest enemy—solitude—solitude that I foresee around my disgrace. I've never lived alone, my captain, I am nothing at all alone. I've employed my life to make some friends from whom I hoped one day to receive support. Poverty, I don't fear, I've often foreseen it in the midst of all my triumphs. I will never be poor with friends like La Fontaine, Moliere—but on top of poverty, there will be solitude, exile, prison. Oh, if you knew how alone I am in this moment, sir—and how to me, you who will soon separate me from all I love,— seem the image of solitude, nothingness—death!

D'ARTAGNAN

Good! You are exaggerating things; at bottom the King loves you.

FOUQUET

Yes—cruelly.

D'ARTAGNAN

Only one day or another he will ruin you.

FOUQUET

I defy him to do that—I'm already ruined.

D'ARTAGNAN

Well, I see with pleasure that you take the thing in good part. You belong to posterity Mr. Fouquet—having played a great role in the history of your times, and you don't have the right to lessen it. Here, look at me, I who seem to exercise superiority over you because I arrested you. Fate which distributes their roles to actors in this world has given me a less beautiful a less agreeable role to play them yours was. You've abused money, you've commanded, you've played all things; as for me, I've dragged my reins, I've obeyed, I've suffered. Well, little as I approved you, sir, the memory of the little I've done, spurs me like a goad and prevents me from bending my old head too soon. I will be atop a good cavalry horse and I will fall rigid still living after having indeed chosen my role.

Do like me, Mr. Fouquet, you will find yourself less ill—this only happens once to men like you—to fall—for the fall from so high that they are destroyed by the flow—the thing is too choose one's role, as I told you, when it happens. There's a later proverb whose words I've forgotten but whose sense I recall for my whole life I've meditated on it. "The end crowns the work."

FOUQUET

That's a fine sermon!

D'ARTAGNAN

A Musketeer's sermon, Milord.

FOUQUET

You love me then, you tell me all this?

D'ARTAGNAN

Perhaps.

(one hears shouts outside: long live the King)

Here's the King without doubt—what do I see? Mr. d'Herblay

at the King's side?

(Aramis, entering, paper in hand.)

FOUQUET

Aramis.

ARAMIS

(to Fouquet)

Yes, me, Milord—I who bring you liberty!

FOUQUET

I am free.

D'ARTAGNAN

Oh—oh—what's that?

ARAMIS

(to D'Artagnan)

Order of the King—indeed!

FOUQUET

To whom do I owe this sudden reversal?

D'ARTAGNAN

And inexplicable.

ARAMIS

To me.

FOUQUET

To you?

D'ARTAGNAN

How's it happen you've become the favorite of the King—you who've never spoken two words to him in your life?

ARAMIS

My friends, you think I've seen the King only twice, while I've seen him often—very often—only we hid it—that's all.

D'ARTAGNAN

I don't understand.

ARAMIS

My dear D'Artagnan—go to the King—here—There he is in the gallery; ask him if this order is indeed real.

D'ARTAGNAN

But—

ARAMIS

Go, go! What the devil! Don't you see His Majesty—?

D'ARTAGNAN

Indeed—in person—I'm going there. I'm going there. This is fine—but the devil take me if I understand any of it.

(returns Fouquet his sword and leaves)

FOUQUET

My word, my dear d'Herblay, I confess to you that me neither—I absolutely understand nothing of what's happening? Will you explain it to me, finally?

ARAMIS

Yes—in short. You were just arrested as a betrayer of your office, you were going to be judged by the parliament as an embezzler—as a thief, you would have been condemned to exile, prison, perhaps to death.

FOUQUET

Well?

ARAMIS

Well—now you are free.

FOUQUET

But how?

ARAMIS

Mr. Colbert was growing great, the King hated you; Mr. Colbert is now only a clerk and the King loves you.

FOUQUET

Speak clearly or I'll go mad.

ARAMIS

Do you recall the birth of Louis XIV?

FOUQUET

Like yesterday.

ARAMIS

Didn't you hear anything said about this birth?

FOUQUET

Nothing, except that he really might not be the son of Louis XIII.

ARAMIS

That's not it; didn't you hear it said that the queen gave birth to twins?

FOUQUET

Never!

ARAMIS

It was so.

FOUQUET

And so—?

ARAMIS

They suppressed one of the two twins; they put him in the Bastille.

FOUQUET

And the other?

ARAMIS

The other one they put on the throne. The two twins resembled each other to such a degree that their mother would be deceived—and is being deceived at this moment.

FOUQUET

Fine! Fine! You were counting on me to help you repair the wrong done to the poor brother of Louis XIV? You really thought I would help you; thanks d'Herblay, thanks!

ARAMIS

That's not it at all.

FOUQUET

Then you went to find the King when you learned the news of my arrest, you begged him, he refused to hear you—you threatened to reveal the secret and Louis XIV overwhelmed, granted to this threat what he refused your generous intercession. I understand—I understand—you hold the King.

ARAMIS

You don't understand the least in the world.

FOUQUET

Then what do you mean?

ARAMIS

What do I mean? I mean the King who was ruining you, the King who hates you, the King who was having you arrested, who was going to deliver you to exile, to prison—perhaps to death—that one has vanished into the depths of the deepest cells of the Château de Vaux and tomorrow will disappear even more profoundly still—for he will return to the Bastille under the name of Marchiali—that is to say his brother.

FOUQUET

While his brother—?

ARAMIS

Well, why you see him, it's he who just ordered your liberty—it's he who instead of imprisoning you is going to enrich you—instead of degrading you is going to cover you with honors—make you great among the great, duke, prince—whatever you like finally.

FOUQUET

Just heaven—and who has managed this horrible deed?

ARAMIS

Me.

FOUQUET

You have dethroned the King? You've imprisoned him?

ARAMIS

Yes.

FOUQUET

And this machination took place here?

ARAMIS

Yes, right here—in this room.

FOUQUET

At Vaux—in my home?

ARAMIS

At Vaux—in your home—for Vaux is especially yours since Mr. Colbert can no longer steal it from you.

FOUQUET

In my home, this crime?

ARAMIS

This crime?

FOUQUET

This abominable crime! This crime more execrable than a murder—this crime which forever dishonors my name and dooms me to the horror of posterity.

ARAMIS

You are delirious, sir—you are speaking too loud, take care.

FOUQUET

I will shout so loud that the universe will hear me.

ARAMIS

Mr. Fouquet! Be careful!

FOUQUET

Yes, you have dishonored me by committing this treason—this attempt against one who was reposing peacefully under my roof. Oh! Misfortune to you!

ARAMIS

Misfortune to the one who under your roof, meditated the ruin of your fortune—of your life!

FOUQUET

He was my guest—he was my King.

ARAMIS

Am I dealing with an idiot?

FOUQUET

You are dealing with an honest man!

ARAMIS

Fool!

FOUQUET

A man who prefers to kill you than let you consummate his dishonor.

(drawing his sword)

ARAMIS

Fool!

(The superintendent hurls the sword.)

FOUQUET

Sir, it would be nicer for me to die here so as not to survive to my shame. If you still have some friendship for me, I beg you—give me death. You say nothing?

ARAMIS

Consider all that awaits us, this justice being done, the King still lives, and his imprisonment saves your life.

FOUQUET

You really tried to act in my interest—so be it—but I cannot accept your service. Still, I don't wish to ruin you; you are going to leave this house—I am responsible for all, you will not be sacrificed any more than he whose ruin you plotted.

ARAMIS

You will be ruined—you—you will be ruined!

FOUQUET

I accept the prophecy—but nothing will stop me. You are going to leave Vaux, you are going to leave France. I give you four hours to put yourself beyond the King's reach.

ARAMIS

Four hours?

FOUQUET

It's more than enough for you to embark and reach Belle-Isle that I gave you for refuge.

ARAMIS

Ah!

FOUQUET

Belle Isle will be for you as Vaux is for the King—so long as I live not a single hair on your head will fall. Go!

ARAMIS

Oh—misfortune!

FOUQUET

Get going! Let's both run—you to save your life—me to save my honor!

ARAMIS

(falling annihilated into an armchair)

Ah! Fouquet, your honesty destroys me—your generosity kills me.

(Fouquet leaves precipitously—Porthos appears a few moments later.)

ARAMIS

Porthos—you were there? You heard? Ah?

PORTHOS

So here we are embroiled with Louis XIV and I thought I was serving the true King!

ARAMIS

Pardon, Porthos, I deceived you, but I will take it all on myself.

PORTHOS

What are you saying, friend?

ARAMIS

No, no, I pray you—let me do it. No untimely devotion! You knew nothing of my plans—you did nothing by yourself. As for me, it's different. I alone am the author of the plot. I had need of my inseparable companion; I called you and you came to me—remembering our old slogan "All for one, one for all". My crime, dear Porthos, was that of being an egoist.

PORTHOS

There's a word I like—since you acted only for yourself it will be impossible for me to bear you a grudge for it—it's so natural.

ARAMIS

Ah! Porthos, in the presence of your naive grandeur—how small I find myself—but what to do? How to decide?

PORTHOS

Let's go to Belle Isle and we will entrench ourselves in the grotto of Locmaria with a barrel of gun powder. If they come after us—we'll light it and will make a sepulcher of broken rocks—of fallen mountains. This will be a splendid funeral. The funeral of giants. Come, Aramis, come.

(They leave by the left.)

(The Queen enters with Colbert and ladies of the Court.)

QUEEN

Truly, Mr. Colbert, I don't understand anything that's going on. Mr. Fouquet returned to favor and Mr. d'Herblay became Prime Minster and Miss de la Vallière, the favorite of yesterday banished abruptly from the court—I'm lost!

COLBERT

Let's wait, Madame; the explanation of all these mysteries won't be long delayed.

LOUISE

(entering)

My word! Where are all these rumors coming from?

(stopping)

Ah! The Queen.

QUEEN

What gives you the boldness to present yourself here, Madame? Moreover, you arrive marvelously to learn the role His Majesty intends to take regarding you.

LOUISE

Madame—pardon—what do you mean?

QUEEN

I mean you are gong to be returned to your family, the order is formal.

LOUISE

You are saying, Madame, that the King—

QUEEN

Well, yes, it's the King—

LOUISE

(joining her hands)

Oh! My God! Why it's impossible—

QUEEN

Eh! Miss—it's very useless to join your hands—but as submissive as you seem to the King of Heaven, it becomes you to do so to the will of earthly princes! So, I repeat to you—obey the order which enjoins you to retire to Blois.

LOUISE

What?—after all that happened right here—after all he told me? This is a terrible dream! No—I really heard! But—then he doesn't love me, he never loved me—what am I saying? He scorns me to the point of abandoning me to a shameful expulsion. Oh, Louis! Louis!

(to the Queen)

Madame, I obey—only be so kind as to tell the King, your son, that I have a broken heart—that I cannot understand—that I am really suffering—but that I pardon him the wrong he is doing me—tell him that after sacrificing myself to a King who abandons me and forgets me—I am going to consecrate myself to God who never abandons those who never forget him—

D'ARTAGNAN

(coming from the right and announcing) The King.

(Enter Marchiali.)

FOUQUET

(coming from the left and announcing the King)

(Enter Louis XIV.)

QUEEN

(looking to the right and the left and uttering a scream)

Ah!

(Marchiali recoils in terror.)

KING

It seems that all the world has forgotten his King.

(pointing to Marchiali)

Captain D'Artagnan—do your duty!

QUEEN

(going to the King, begging)

Louis! Louis!

D'ARTAGNAN

(going to Marchiali)

Sir, you are my prisoner!

BLACKOUT

ACT V
SCENE 9

The Grotto of Locmaria.

ARAMIS

You recognize it, Porthos?

PORTHOS

By my word. We are in the grotto of Locmaria.

ARAMIS

Yes, foreseeing the disastrous issue of the battle that we just received at the hands of the King's men. I had a boat prepared and gave a rendezvous to three men.

PORTHOS

Aramis, I think we ought to have gotten ourselves killed on the rampart.

ARAMIS

And what use would our death have been?

PORTHOS

So as not to flee, so as not to be obliged to hide ourselves like foxes in this hole.

(he staggers)

ARAMIS

What's wrong, Porthos?

PORTHOS

My friend—a weakness is taking me.

ARAMIS

Well, set down on this log I am going to give our men the agreed signal, and help them put the punt in the sea.

PORTHOS

Go, dear Aramis, you are all wisdom and all prudence.

(Aramis makes the sound of an owl—and is responded to with the cry of screech owl)

ARAMIS

(on the side opposite Porthos)

You are there Jonathos?

JONATHOS

Eight muskets, 5000 rounds and a barrel of gunpowder—yes,

Milord.

ARAMIS

Fine—let's begin by pulling the canoe. Take it from this grotto—then we'll put it in the water.

(Exit Aramis.)

PORTHOS

(alone)

Decidedly, I think I was right to make my will—I feel—and for the first time— In my family there's a tradition on this subject—when our legs fail—our death is near—

(trying to stand)

As for me—today is unusual—I can hardly remain standing.

(the baying of hounds and trumpets can be heard)

ARAMIS

Porthos!

PORTHOS

What?

ARAMIS

Listen.

(you can hear voices—tally ho! tally ho! tally ho!)

PORTHOS

You'd say huntsmen.

ARAMIS

Have you seen passing like a shadow?

PORTHOS

What shadow?

ARAMIS

A fox!

PORTHOS

By God! Nothing surprising. You recall, Aramis, when you were hunting, the animals always come to hole up in this grotto.

ARAMIS

(seizing Porthos arm)

Porthos!

PORTHOS

Well?

ARAMIS

Do you see them?

PORTHOS

Oh—huntsmen.

ARAMIS

No, by god! But King's guards, who in beating the land, raised a fox, followed it into the grotto, and are trying to figure out how it got in. Porthos if they enter, they will discover us—we are cursed then! For we are lost.

PORTHOS

They're approaching—I see them—good—only a dozen.

ARAMIS

(giving an iron bar to Porthos)

Porthos—quickly to the canoes—pull it to the sea—we will lie in ambush here –we will defend; the entrance to the grotto until you've floated the bark—

PORTHOS

Saving your opinion, Aramis, I think it would be better for me to remain here with this crowbar—as they enter, I'll let my iron bar fall on this skulls. It's a way of killing them, one after another, discretely and without noise—what do you say of the plan? You smile?

ARAMIS

Excellent, dear friend.

PORTHOS

And then, because there are only a few of them the thing can be done in two or three minutes.

(Confused voices outside.)

PORTHOS

(low)

Aramis, they're coming in.

ARAMIS

Well, strike.

(He goes off. Music during which ones hears the heavy blows of the bar striking the skulls and the choked cries of those who fall.)

A VOICE

Treason! Get back—get back—Comrades—now fire.

(shots)

PORTHOS

Not touched. Ha! Ha!

ARAMIS

(returning with a barrel of powder)

Well?

PORTHOS

Look—

ARAMIS

(consulting)

Ah—they've beaten a retreat; they are consulting in the distance.

PORTHOS

Let 'em come. I'm waiting for them.

ARAMIS

Porthos, take this barrel to which I've attached a fuse. Wait till our enemies are only a few feet from you and hurl it in their midst. Can you do it?

PORTHOS

(lifting the barrel with one hand)

By God—it hardly weighs a hundred pounds.

ARAMIS

You've clearly understood.

PORTHOS

Fine! When you explain to me, I always understand. Give me the tinder.

ARAMIS

Here—here it is—Hurl the tinder, my Jupiter, and we will rejoin you.

(Exit Aramis.)

PORTHOS

Don't worry!

(The trumpet and drum can be heard.)

PORTHOS

Good, there they are.

(he hurls the barrel)

(The drums cease to beat. The clarion sounds—shouts can be heard. "Cut the fuse. Cut the fuse!")

ARAMIS

(from afar)

Come—come Porthos!

PORTHOS

(trying in vain to flee)

Yes—yes—there's my fatigue taking me again—I can no longer walk—what's to be said?

ARAMIS

(in the distance)

Quick! Quick! Porthos.

PORTHOS

Go, go—I'm coming—impossible, I am a dead man!

ARAMIS

(from afar)

The barrel is going to explode—in the name of heaven—come.

VOICES

(off)

Bear up, Milord.

(the barrel explodes. The rocks fall on Porthos)

PORTHOS

(after having tried for a moment to raise the rocks, falls back crushed under their weight)

Ah—too heavy.

(after he's crushed, Aramis can be seen rowing away)

D'ARTAGNAN

(arriving on the scene followed by some Musketeers)

Mercy! Mercy! In the name of the King! Porthos! Porthos! Bad luck—he is no more—the giant sleeps the eternal sleep in the sepulcher that God made for his body.

CURTAIN

ABOUT THE AUTHOR

Frank J. Morlock has written and translated many plays since retiring from the legal profession in 1992. His translations have also appeared on Project Gutenberg, the Alexandre Dumas Père web page, Literature in the Age of Napoléon, Infinite Artistries.com, and Munsey's (formerly Blackmask). In 2006 he received an award from the North American Jules Verne Society for his translations of Verne's plays. He lives and works in México.

www.ingramcontent.com/pod-product-compliance
Lightning Source LLC
Chambersburg PA
CBHW032105090426
42743CB00007B/236